To Be Frank

One Man's Journey
Through Cancer

NIC COLLINS

Published in 2021 by Discover Your Bounce Publishing

www.discoveryourbouncepublishing.com

ISBN 978-1-914428-04-3

Although the author and publisher have made every effort to
ensure that the information in this book is correct at the time of
going to print, the author and publisher do not assume and
therefore disclaim liability to any party. The author and the
publisher will not be held responsible for any loss or damage
save for that caused by their negligence.

Although the author and the publisher have made every
reasonable attempt to achieve accuracy in the content of this
book, they assume no responsibility for errors or omissions.

Page design and typesetting by Discover Your Bounce
Publishing

To my dad for the last lesson that he left us.

Francis Johnstone Collins

(1929 – 1998)

"Frank"

TO BE FRANK

iv

CONTENTS

THE FIRST JOURNEY

"You can sit up now Mr Collins, pop your pants and your trousers back up and when you are ready, take a seat over there."

I do as instructed and place myself in a cheap looking plastic, brown, bucket style chair, the type you see in school dining halls and waiting rooms.

Someone else walks into the room after a short knock on the door, mutters something that I cannot comprehend, passes over a beige cardboard file, and walks over to the farthest corner of the room. It feels a little like I am in the middle of a job interview as the guy now holding the file scans its contents and then, whilst still standing in front of me, addresses me directly.

"Well, the cystoscopy (that's a tiny camera inserted through the eye of your penis) shows no obvious problems in and around your bladder or urinary system, so the bleeding that you experienced we believe was probably just a polyp (a small group of tissue that's torn) and nothing to cause any real concern. I checked your prostate just for good measure, at the same time (a rubber-gloved finger inserted in your anus) and that all feels as it should."

I visibly relax when he hits me with the follow-up. "However, the ultrasound (a handheld scan over the stomach area on a cold gel) we performed on you a little earlier shows a seven-centimetre lesion on your right kidney, it's cancer and it's going to need to come out, so the next time you hear from us will be to come in for a full CT scan (chest and abdominal x-ray) so don't ignore it, any questions?"

I will never forget the way I received this truly life changing diagnosis. It's so matter-of-fact, it puts me completely on the back foot and in that moment I cannot think of anything relevant to say. "You can go now."

I thank him for his time and leave the room, working my way through the corridors, ignoring the lift and walking down the stairs through the exit and into the fresh air. Breathe!

As I walk towards my car, parked in an open-air space about four hundred yards away, my mind starts to clear. I light up a cigarette, take a lungful in and exhale. What in the hell just happened? Did he really say cancer? How am I going to tell my wife? What about my kids? Am I going to die? No, I am too young to die, aren't I? This cannot be happening, not to me!

Three weeks before all this drama, late in February 2015, an early morning at work marked the beginning of this story. I work (at the time of writing this, I still do) for a large car dealership as one of its sales advisors. It is a job I have been doing for about three years and really enjoy, not just for the thrill of the sale or its financial rewards but because it means getting to meet and talk to new people every day, finding out a little about their lives and hopefully advising them on the correct vehicle for their future needs before they spend what is still, for most people, a huge amount of money. Every morning we have a sales meeting which sets the tone for the day and the upcoming week. Once this is over, the sales staff go outside onto the pitch and check all of the cars. Open the boots, check the price boards are in the cars and are correctly priced, and move them around or straighten up the lines. With such a large pitch, this takes all eight of us about 45 minutes to complete and on this particular morning it takes even longer as we had an overnight frost and all of the windscreens need to be cleared. There is a truly beautiful blue clear sky; the sun is bright but low and it's freezing out here. You can see your breath in front of your face. I have on a padded ski style jacket, provided by the company with its insignia, I also have a pair of leather gloves on which the other guys take the mickey out of. They call them my cat burglar gloves, however it's me that has the last laugh as we are opening freezing wet doors and boots and normal woollen gloves get soaking wet and are of no use when trying to stay dry and warm.

Once we are all finished, we go about our days. We return all the keys to the secure area they are kept in and crack on. As any guy will tell you, for some reason being exposed to the freezing cold for any amount of time generally results in needing a wee, pronto! This is certainly the case for me that morning and I leg it into the gents toilet on the ground floor. Coat unzipped, flies down, adjustment of boxers and phew, just made it! My relief is very short-lived as I look down into the urinal bowl I'm leaning against to see bright red blood pouring out where normally urine would be. It looks like somebody has got a bottle of red wine and is pouring the whole thing away.

It takes me a moment to realise what I'm witnessing and the possible significance of it. I clean up, get myself together and find a quiet spot to call my local doctors surgery and book an appointment for as soon as possible which was the beginning of the following week.

I am not a doctor person, never have been. I just do not go. I put up with things, tough them out. I hate taking pills. It's in my upbringing, both my older brother and I are the same. Our old man was what you call a proper 'man's man', very rarely would you ever see him ill, you'd never see him go to the doctors. I remember as a kid, the occasional times where he would have a really bad cold or even flu, he would take himself off to bed on a night-time with a plastic washing up bowl filled with boiling water and Vickes vapour rub with a towel over his head and sweat it out. I do not remember him ever having a day off work for any illness.

You may think if that is the case, why did you call your doctors straight away? Well, my dad died of cancer of the colon. It wasn't picked up until it was too late and had he reacted to the early warning signs, he may well have had a lot more time. He passed away late in 1998, having just turned sixty-nine. He had had the diagnosis for about a year. Born in 1929, at the start of the great depression under the reign of King George V, it was a vastly different time. He was the eldest of six, three boys and three girls, all living in a three-bedroomed, red brick, semi-detached council house with an outside toilet and sharing a tin bath in front the fire on a Sunday night. He had to share a bed with his two other brothers, they had one set of sheets that had to be washed and dried on the same day and the bedroom walls were lined with newspapers. As the Second World War broke out, his old fella and old lady could not wait to get rid of them. They were evacuated. My dad and his oldest brother managed to stay together and were taken in by a couple in Dawlish where they remained until it was safe to return to the larger cities and towns.

Because my dad's dad was a steel erector, he was exempt from active service during the war. This left him and his wife to continue their miserable, selfish existence, drinking themselves into a near stupor and creating even more children that they could find new ways to ignore. Dad left school at fourteen (that was normal in those days) and followed in the footsteps of his father as a lot of boys did. He became a steel erector and in no time was as good if not better than his old man. Because Dad had no fear working three hundred feet plus up in the air with no safety harness (no real health and safety in those days), he was always in demand. His career was interrupted for a couple of years with the onset of National Service where he served as a logistics driver. The British Army put him through his driving test (he was the most impatient driver in the world!) and he did his time here in the UK. He never spoke much of it; I remember as a little boy trying to glean information out of him as growing up in the seventies with all those John Wayne war films, I was fascinated by the war and the British Armed Forces in particular, as lots of young boys are. He told me that his time in the army certainly was not glamorous, he drove lorries and occasionally ran messages by motorbike. He said he used to box on a Friday night in the sergeant's mess for a pint of beer and a cheese sandwich as a treat! Can you imagine?

Being the stoic person that he was, when he first discovered blood in his stools and suffered pain in his rectum, he put it down to piles which is something a lot of people get, particularly if they spend lots of time sitting on cold surfaces such as steel as he would have. He only retired in August 1994, aged sixty-five. I am not sure when he first had symptoms, he never shared this with Mum and certainly not with my older brother or me. Bear in mind even in the late nineties, the internet was not in every household and there were certainly no smartphones. You can't just type it in like now and have an instant diagnosis, and by the time he realised something was really not right, it was just too late.

That is why I called the doctors straight away. That night, once we had settled the girls into bed, I sat my wife down to tell her what had happened. She is a little shocked at first, I assure her I have made an appointment and promise I will attend. As you do these days, we go straight to Google and I am immediately convinced I have testicular cancer. During the following week, I have no repeat of the bleeding, no pain anywhere, just a nagging feeling that something horrible is going to happen which I keep to myself and I continue to be upbeat. Michelle (my wife), knowing what I am like, makes me promise that although everything seems fine now, that I will still go and get checked out.

Sitting in the doctors surgery, I must confess I feel a bit of a fraud. The bleeding had been a week ago, I haven't had any recurrence and was in no pain. I explain what had happened to my doctor (not that I had seen her before) and she gives me a full examination. She takes my blood pressure, a blood sample, a urine sample and asks me the usual questions about my family history, smoking, drinking, diet and exercise. All seems fine but due to my age (forty-eight) she refers me to have a cystoscopy and an ultrasound just as a precaution.

It takes about a week for the appointment to come through the post and it is in another weeks' time. For Michelle and me, it is like time is standing still. I can see the mounting worry in her face, the way she looks at the girls and how she speaks carefully about future events. I do my best to carry on as normal, as is my way. We discuss it in our private time occasionally, I am positive it will not dominate our thoughts, certainly not mine. Let's just wait until something gets confirmed and then we will deal with it.

Bang! So now it's confirmed, we are back to where I started this story. I am leaning against my shiny new demo (company car), drawing back heavily on a cigarette thinking, what the hell am I going to say to Michelle? She is waiting on my call. And what about the girls? At this time they are aged fourteen and ten.

I reluctantly make the call; Michelle is just about to collect our youngest from primary school and I try to fob her off, telling her we will talk about it later. She won't have it, so I have to hear her heart breaking over the phone, it is awful. I am standing in a public car park with tears streaming down my face and I tell her not to worry for now, to get herself together, sort out the girls, I am on my way home and we will sort it all out later. I remember standing there for about another ten minutes or so while I chain-smoked another couple of cigarettes, getting my thoughts together. Driving home, I make the decision that this will have as little impact as possible and that I will come out the other side. I am not going to feel sorry for myself and I certainly don't want anyone else's pity, bugger that!

Later that evening, I recount everything that had happened that afternoon. Michelle was horrified at the way the news was delivered to me (strangely, when I tell people how I was first diagnosed, I now find it amusing) and she hung on every word. We had to wait for the Urology department at Southmead Hospital in Bristol, where we live, to get in touch.

Now time really is standing still. We make the decision not to tell anybody for now. I will have to tell my immediate boss as I am going to be needing some more time off for further appointments and tests etc. The next morning, I speak to my boss. He is very sympathetic, as you might expect, and tells me whatever I need, just do it and keep him in the loop.

To some point I inherited my impatience from my old fella. I hate waiting for anything – you should see me trying to get a beer at a crowded bar and my brother is even worse! It's been around a week, no letter. I make a doctor's appointment and I am surprised by the fact I don't have to wait, they will squeeze me in the following day. Different doctor this time, he looks at his computer monitor and catches up with me and I explain to him that I am concerned that no one has been in touch. He makes a call there and then, right in front of me, and gets the appropriate department. He assures me it's all in-hand and I should have my appointment letter the following day. At this point, after checking his screen again, he sees that I am down as a smoker and strongly advises me to give up as soon as possible as this will give me a greater chance of my blood clotting, helping me to recover from what is going to be major surgery. I leave the surgery, drive to the McDonalds near where I work, order a coffee, stand in the morning sun, smoke two cigarettes, bin the rest of the packet and my lighter, and I have not had one since, after being a smoker for the best part of thirty-five years. I have to say, I do not know how anyone can say they have or have had cancer and then keep smoking, even though I am assured my having smoked was not linked to my cancer. The next day, Michelle calls me at work to say the date for the CT scan has arrived, it's in two weeks' time. This, for Michelle, is a complete nightmare. She knows that not only did my dad die relatively early with cancer but so did his next brother down, his oldest sister and the middle one, all before their sixties. You could say it runs in my family!

Being a bit of a pragmatist (Michelle would say a control freak), I am now all-consumed by thoughts of whether there be enough money to see Michelle and the girls through if the very worst were to happen. I contact my 'guy' who looks after my meagre finances.

We sit over a coffee and a bacon sandwich while he goes through my portfolio. He assures me that my life insurance cover would pay out immediately and the private pension that I have had since I was twenty would also pay out a full dividend to Michelle, and that my family would be financially sound. Knowing that I had all my ducks in a row was a massive comfort to me, it meant it was something that I did not need to worry about.

It's early April 2015 now, almost four weeks since my original diagnosis, time is standing still for both Michelle and me. Still, nobody knows about my cancer and to add to the stress of this, the girls are both getting really excited as we have a once in a lifetime holiday booked in late July to Disney World, Florida, staying at one of the Disney hotels. At this stage, I am honestly more concerned with the fact that I might have to tell them we cannot go rather than the fact that I have stage three cancer that needs an operation.

The day of the scan comes (at last). Michelle insists on coming with me and to be honest, I am more than a little relieved that she does. We drive across town to the hospital and arrive with plenty of time. Southmead Hospital has recently been rebuilt and it's like walking through a modern-day airport with little stores and coffee shops dotted along the main concourse. We book in through a cash point style machine that scans the number on your appointment letter and it directs us to the department we need. We find it, find a human behind a small reception desk and book in. We are advised to take a seat, someone will come and call me soon. After about 20 minutes, a nurse appears and calls my name. At this point Michelle cannot accompany me any further because of the radiation precautions around the x-ray department.

I follow the nurse through the security door and get directed to a changing room where I am instructed to remove everything except my pants, put on the robe that is hanging on a hook in there and load all of my belongings into a wire shopping basket. Once changed you walk out with your basket (but not with your dignity) and sit on another of those plastic bucket chairs in a draughty corridor while you wait for the yellow radiation caution signs to go out and you then get invited in. The radiologist does their best to make you feel at ease, directs you to deposit your basket down out of the way, beckons you to lay down on the movable bed within the scanner and asks you if you have had one before? They then explain what is about to happen. My scan today (and all of them since) is twofold. I get sent through the scanner twice to start with then they insert a dye into me which is called 'with contrast' and I go through twice more. So, before they can start the process, I must lie down with my left arm extended behind my head. They then insert a canula into my arm and attach a line that the dye is going to pass through. Once this is completed, and every time I have had this done since, they compliment me on my tattoos. They leave the room and the scanner starts up. It sounds like a giant washing machine, there is a loud click and suddenly you are on your way towards what I can only describe as a giant white POLO mint! Before you go through it tells you to breathe in and hold, backed up by a lit cartoon style sign directly above you, and after a few seconds it gives the command to breathe normally, which comes as a mighty relief. This is repeated and then the radiologist comes over the speaker to tell you that the dye is about to go into your arm. There's a swishing water noise and you then head back through the scanner with the same set of instructions for another two goes. I have had the best part of a dozen of these scans at the time of writing this, in fact I have one booked for next week, and when the dye goes in and I pass through the scanner I always get exactly the same sensations of a really strong metallic taste in my mouth and throat and a burning feeling in my nether regions. It only lasts literally a couple of seconds but it's not a nice experience. After that the bed draws backwards to where you started, the machine whirring starts to slow down until it stops, there's a click as the door gets released and the radiologist appears and removes the line from the canula. Once you have gotten dressed, they ask you to sit and wait for a little while and then they remove the canula. Before that, the radiologist explains the scans will be sent to the consultant and they will get them in a couple of weeks, and at that point you are free to go as long as you feel ok.

That's it.

The two weeks comes and goes I have major concerns that it has been almost two months since my original bleeding, so I decide to start calling the Urology department at Southmead and find out what is going on. I eventually get through to my consultant's secretary who informs me that my case is due for discussion within the team, which they do every week on a Wednesday morning. Today is Tuesday so it looks like I am in luck. She calls me back on my mobile the following afternoon, asking me if I am available to come in Thursday afternoon at two-thirty to meet with the consultant. I confirm that I will be there and call Michelle with the news. She insists on coming with me and makes arrangements with a good friend to look after the girls after school for an hour or so.

So, once again we are sat in a waiting area. This one is huge, it's like being in an airport terminal. All the seats are facing a long wall with a huge TV monitor flashing up people's names with directions of which ward they should then proceed to. After only 5 minutes or so there it is, my name in lights. As I stand I can sense everybody else looking at me, all probably wondering, "What is wrong with him?" We walk through an adjoining corridor to another much smaller waiting area based within the Urology department. There are lots of posters depicting all sorts of illnesses that are the undertaking of this department, for some reason I am drawn to the prostate and erectile disfunction ones that adorn the whole of the opposite wall and bizarrely, start to worry if all the people sat there already waiting are wondering if that's why I am there. As we huddle and talk softly, some people around us are getting called in and others are leaving having seen their own practitioner. A largish chap comes out and calls my name, we follow him into the inner sanctum where introductions are made. He explains that he is the main guy and I immediately know I am in trouble! The leading consultant in the country is going to be operating on me, sod it, although thinking about it, I must be in safe hands if the top man is looking after me. That's it, let's be positive. He asks me if I know why I am here, seeming to want to check my understanding of what is going on. I answer positively and any concerns he may have had in talking to me disappear. He explains the results of the scan to us. I have a renal cell carcinoma, which is residing on my right kidney, it's rather large which means the kidney will have to be removed. He explains the procedure, assures us I only need one kidney anyway and tells us he would like to operate sooner rather than later. As he has some free time on his private list, he can get me into the Spire Private Hospital but on the NHS. He is careful to make light of it, making it sound like as he has the time we might as well just get on with it. We found out later that it was actually quite critical and I can tell you now, by the time I actually went in for my operation, I was going through boxes of painkillers like they were Smarties. Without a doubt, had I not made that initial call to my doctors, it would have been too late by the time I couldn't tolerate the pain anymore and realised something was really wrong. Michelle asks whether I will need any chemotherapy or radiotherapy after the operation and he assures us that neither of these will be of any benefit, I have one of the few cancers that do not respond to that type of therapy. We pepper him with whatever questions our numbed minds can think of as we are both thinking, bloody hell, this is happening in just over a week. He was a genuinely nice guy, not only did he put us both at ease but I truly believe without a doubt that he saved my life at that time.

We leave full of hope and at the same time, I will admit it, scared stiff. We head to the nearest Greggs, get some coffees and a sausage roll for me (it's the law). As we sit in the car, we make plans to tell people that we care about what's been happening, but we have to start with the girls first, something that we are dreading. Facing the girls and giving them the news with the words "Dad's got cancer" is without doubt the worst thing I have ever had to do, seeing their little faces and their tears welling up was just awful. Together we put the most positive slant on it we could, it was all good news as it had been found early, the doctor was really positive the operation would be ok and you only need one kidney anyway. There are lots of people out there with only one kidney. I promised them I would be fine and after a couple of months rest, we will be going on holiday to Disney and I could not wait. Thank goodness we had that holiday booked, it got us out of the crap! There was some concern over the timings as I was booked into the Spire for the fifth of May and you are not supposed to fly for at least the next 10 weeks and that's if there are no complications. We worked it out, it was ten weeks and two days, we're bloody going!

Michelle told me later that both the girls were devastated but didn't want to show their feelings in front of me as they thought it would make me sad (which it would have) and they both in turn cried their hearts out a bit later, wrapped around our chocolate Labrador with Michelle. To a great degree I left Michelle to tell who she thought needed to know, although I called my big brother and my two closest friends to give them the news. It's such a difficult conversation to have but they all came up trumps as I knew they would, anything we need, just call they said. The following morning, in work, I had to tell all my colleagues which, after having a quick conversation with the boss, we did in the morning meeting. To be fair, I found it quite difficult to tell them but I managed to keep my emotions in check.

They were all shocked but supportive, they were a good bunch and the guy who had been responsible for my initial training made light of it as we departed to go and sort out the pitch as usual. He shouted out, "Mind the way, dead man walking," which immediately cracked us all up. All of the customers sitting in the waiting area looked at us bemused and that was it, awkwardness sorted. Well done, mate.

It's hard to believe that I am going in for a major medical procedure in less than ten days. During the lead up to the operation I begin to think seriously about the possibility of not coming through it. It is planned to be a keyhole procedure lasting around four hours under a general anaesthetic, I have not experienced anything like this before. A couple of things creep into my head. If I did not make it, Michelle was still a relatively young, attractive woman. It would not be fair for me to think of her being on her own for the rest of her life. Then comes the thought of another man bringing up my girls, which is unbearable. I cannot believe this horrible, crappy disease could put me in such a vulnerable position, that ain't happening! I'm the alpha male in the girls' lives, I'm their protector, they are my little cubs, it's my job to guide them and help them to realise right from wrong, that they always have choices, to be their own person. Here I am, years later and sometimes I think I have done too good a job with them, they are fiercely independent, do not suffer fools gladly and know exactly what they want. As I write this, I am so proud of them, I am beaming!

It's the Tuesday the week before my operation, I am home as it is my day off (we work alternate weekend days), the house is quiet as Michelle is in work and the girls are at school. It's just me and the hound and, at this moment, she is crashed out on our bed upstairs. I spend all morning writing letters by hand to all the people I love and care for, just in case. I know it sounds a bit morbid and dramatic but let us be realistic, there is a fair chance that I may not recover. I record a farewell message on my iPhone. I am crying as I complete this task but again, it's a control thing for me and once I have completed it I feel better about myself.

There's just three days to go and it's my weekend to be in work, I keep myself busy as usual. It helps to take my mind off things. I had the May Day bank holiday off and spent it with Michelle and the girls. We went off with the dog somewhere and had a Chinese takeaway for tea. With an impending operation you should not have anything to eat or drink for at least 2 hours before. I was due to be in the Spire Hospital at seven in the morning so apart from the pre-operation shakes they give you to have two hours before you come in, you're not allowed anything else. I must confess I do not remember the pre-op meeting for this operation but it turns out there was some sort of issue and I got missed. This was four days before I was due in. I get a call saying they would not be able to perform the operation as I had not had a pre-op. You have got to be bloody kidding, what am I going to say to Michelle and the girls? Sod that, I am coming up to the hospital now and you can do the pre-op today, and that's exactly what happened. They are all pretty much the same, they get you in and take your blood pressure, they take countless vials of blood, hook you up to an ECG machine to record your heart's rhythm and take your temperature. They then issue you with a load of instructions for the day and give you two yummy (not) bottles of a milkshake style drink to take home with you to consume 2 hours before you come in for the op.

I kiss the girls goodnight, tuck them in and promise to see them tomorrow as they are going to come into the hospital the following evening to see me. Night, night, sweet dreams, love you, as was our nightly ritual. Michelle had arranged for one of our closest friends to come in the morning at about six-thirty, which was the time we would need to leave, and help get the girls ready for school.

We go to bed feeling apprehensive about what the next day will bring. We are up early, Michelle fusses over me, makes sure I take the 'shakes' and checks my overnight bag for the umpteenth time. Our good friend is on time, after a brief chat she throws us out of our own home and we drive to the hospital, nervously chatting most of the way. We arrive bang on time and after parking in their private car park, we book in at the reception. It's like being in a posh hotel, after they have taken my details, they ask me what newspaper I would like in the morning. Blimey, I think, I am going to be here tomorrow morning. That was a comforting thought. Once all of the registration is done, I have a wrist band with my name and date of birth attached to both wrists. A nurse is summoned, and she leads us away to my room with Michelle nervously making small talk with her. I have to say the room is lovely, spacious, well-ventilated, bright, and clean, complete with a TV and en suite bathroom. The nurse explains that I am first on the list and that the anaesthetist will pop in shortly. She asks me to get changed into the gown that is draped over my bed and she will be back in a minute.

I do as asked, the nurse returns and fits me with what is commonly referred to as 'flight' socks, long white elasticated leggings that also encompass the end of your feet. They are designed to stop clots developing in your legs following surgery and she informs me that I will need to continue to wear them for at least a couple of weeks after the operation. The anaesthetist then appears, checks my details and date of birth, asks me if I have any allergies and then explains that they will come and get me shortly to take me down to the operating theatre, give me some cool drugs to make me sleep and then get me sorted. Then, to our surprise, he asks me to lift my gown, asks me what side I'm having the operation on, then draws an 'X' on the appropriate spot with a black Sharpie! Michelle and I exchange glances and we aren't sure whether to laugh or go into panic mode.

At this point my consultant sticks his head around the door to check all is ok. As I said before, he is around my age, late forties, around six-foot, a little bit shorter than me and the waistline has thickened somewhat. He is dressed head to foot in brightly coloured Lycra bicycle garb complete with his helmet still in place on his head and pedal cleats attached to his shoes, he is truly a sight to behold. He makes the effort to explain that he has ridden in this morning as he is doing his bit to get fit. He comments on what a lovely day it is out there, reassures me that they will come for me soon and he will see me in theatre shortly. Both he and the anaesthetist leave together and Michelle and I are left to nervously chat and raise each other's spirits. Once again, I tell her not to worry, I'm going to be fine, made of tough stuff, me. She smiles and we embrace and tell each another how much we love one another. She makes fun of me in my backwards fitting gown and my flight socks and takes a photo of me sat in one of those tall, leather visitor chairs, you know, the ones with the pine wood arms (it's on the back cover if you want a laugh).

Shortly after this, the nurse comes in and tells us there is a slight change of plans. They have had to put someone else in front of me on today's list and I won't be going down for about another hour. To be fair it was only an hour but for Michelle and me, it was the longest hour of our lives!

Finally, it's time. A nurse and two porters arrive and explain that they are going to take me down to theatre now. Once again, my arm tags are checked, I am asked my name and date of birth, and with that I am told to get onto the bed which they unhook from its housing. They wheel me out into the corridor, we turn right and head off to the lift. I feel a bit soft at this point because I am perfectly able to walk but my offer is rebuked as this is their system of due diligence and the nurse explains that it stops the possibility of any trips or a fall which could then put the surgery in doubt. The buttons get pressed and as the door opens, the nurse tells Michelle this is as far as she can go. We quickly hug and kiss, utter "I love you" and I am whisked into the lift, the doors close and we are off.

We are now on the theatre floor. As the doors of the lift open, I am met by a little entourage. The anaesthetist smiles and says hello, apologises for the slight delay and introduces the other members of the theatre team and their roles. I am rolled into a little anti-room where, through oblong shaped windows attached to the two doors in front of me, I can clearly see the operating table with huge lights and lots of other standalone machines around it. Once again, I have my arm tags checked, I get asked the same questions including why I am there, and then they ask me to lay in a particular position which will give the easiest access for the surgeon. They put a canula in my right arm, explaining that this is needed for the solution they are about to inject into me to put me to sleep, and they place another one in my opposite hand. One last time I am asked to confirm who I am and my date of birth, whether I have any allergies and if so, what? Everyone is now in gowns with matching hats, face masks and visors. The anaesthetist explains that he is about to put the anaesthesia into me, he asks me to relax and on his command count out loud backwards from ten. The command comes and I don't remember getting to eight! I am relying on Michelle's recollection for the next bit as I am out for the count.

As the lift doors close, it feels like I have just been mugged, I feel so helpless, even abandoned. I remember standing there thinking, now what am I supposed to do? The nurses try their best to smile, reassuring me that he is in good hands and I wander off back to his room. Once inside, I see his perfectly neat slippers put side by side (he only wears them in hospital, he hates slippers full stop), his book and reading glasses on his side table, again left neatly. I go over to the window and look out without really seeing anything. All of a sudden, the room starts to close in on me and I need to get out. I decide on a little walk and end up in the main reception a couple of floors down. My brother is in the city today and he calls me to meet up. I take him up on his offer saying I can't be too long. We head into the city centre, five or so minutes away by car, chatting nervously all the way. We meet up with our parents for a coffee and they all fire questions at me whilst my head is still back in the hospital. After what seems like an eternity, my brother drives me back to the Spire and deposits me back at the reception.

My first enquiry is around twelve-thirty and I am assured that the operation has gone well and he is now in recovery. With some relief I return to his room, willing him to return to me as soon as he can. It takes an age for him to be rolled back in and I am back at the small reception by the lifts waiting when he arrives. I am totally shocked by the sight of him. He is so pale, he looks absolutely dreadful and I have never seen him look like that. It is heartbreaking to see all of these tubes and wires attached to him. I wait patiently for them to put the bed back in place, organise all of the wires and tubes, explain to him about the 'panic' button and check him over (all his vital signs: blood pressure, etc.) before leaving us alone. I manage to lean in and kiss him gently on the cheek, tell him I love him and ask him how he is feeling. Bless him, at this stage he is not really with it so I remind him that I need to go and collect our youngest daughter from school and that there is a meeting for the school camp that she is looking forward to going on. The girls and I will be back in to see him later. Get some rest. He nods and says go and sort the girls out, I will see you all later. He is so tired and looks all in. I thank my lucky stars he is back and race off to sort the girls.

I vaguely remember trying to smile at Michelle as they roll me past her in the little reception area by the nurses' station on my floor. She has tears in her eyes as she asks me if I am ok? She walks alongside my bed as they take me back to my private room. The bed is put back in position, the various monitors and drains are hooked up and tested, and I am given a big 'button' which is explained to me as a 'pain button'. Just squeeze it if I am in any discomfort and someone will be along in an instant. After a bit of pillow plumping and a note written on my chart at the end of my bed, it is just Michelle and me. The relief on her face is palpable and she holds my hand, saying, "welcome back." I don't really recall what was said over the next few minutes, but I know that our youngest needs collecting from primary school and so I encourage her to leave so that I could get some rest. She promises to come back in the evening with the girls so that they could see me.

With everyone gone I slip back to sleep. I remember feeling more a discomfort than any outright pain and spend the rest of the afternoon trying to doze off in between twenty-minute obs (observations). It is truly ironic that they tell you to rest as much as you can as it is really important for you to get well then, just as you fall asleep, someone comes along and wakes you up, asks you your name and date of birth, puts a thermometer in your ear, attaches a tight arm band to check your blood pressure and does a blood sugar test by pricking the end of one of your fingers with a sharp needle! Every twenty minutes! This goes on for pretty much the rest of the afternoon. I can't begin to tell you how relaxing it is – not! Both the consultant surgeon and the anaesthetist come by to express how well the operation has gone and they are both incredibly positive they had got it all. Just rest now!

Sometime around five I am presented with dinner, apparently I had chosen something off their menu in the morning when I was being booked in, not that I can recall. I'm a little queasy so I am not sure if I ate anything on that first evening. Shortly after this,

Michelle turns up with the girls. Unfortunately, they happen to come in just as I am throwing up some bile into one of those cardboard Petri dishes they give you. The girls look at me absolutely horrified. I do my best to smile and reassure them I am ok, just feeling a little bit rough. They both come forward for a kiss and a cuddle and ask me how I am. We talk a little about their days, the youngest one has had a meeting late in the afternoon at her school and was all signed up to go on a school camp in about a month's time and is clearly excited about it. Michelle is treating them to dinner too. They confirm that our dog at home is well and has been taken out and there is nothing to worry about. Michelle can see I am tiring quickly and explains to both of them that, "Dad is fine and we should leave him to rest." We all have a goodnight cuddle and I make them promise to come in and see me tomorrow night, I tell them I will be a lot better by then, after getting a good night's rest. Michelle kisses me goodnight on the forehead and says she will be back in the morning and, "Is there anything you want?" I reply, "No thanks" and off they all go.

I had 'keyhole' surgery performed on me, the surgical team prefer using this method as it leads to a quicker recovery time and far less scarring. It's also far quicker than what they call an 'open procedure'. The chance of any complications or infections are greatly reduced by using this method. As I understand it, they inflated my stomach with gas and insert a camera and the appropriate tools they need to cut away the affected area. Once this is done with a kidney, it is in its own sack/bag with the cancer is attached to the kidney itself and they then extract it down through an incision that they make at the base of the stomach where it meets the pelvis and hips. They told me afterwards that the real work begins once it is removed as they must join all the cut or torn tissue, muscle and blood vessels back together and that sometimes it becomes necessary mid-operation to switch to an 'open procedure' which adds time onto the original operation. Luckily this wasn't the case with me but I ended up taking an hour or so longer than originally planned because it took a while for my body temperature to return in resus. Once they were satisfied with everything, they used metal staples to close the wound rather than stiches which could easily break in the position that they were in. This, again, apparently means less chance of scarring and can easily be removed at the local doctors surgery at the appropriate time.

During that first night in hospital the 'obs' became every 2 hours. It is still frustrating but so much better than before. I manage to go all through the night without pressing my 'panic button'. They have me on painkillers, of course, and they also ply me with laxatives as it's important to get your bowel movements back to normal once you have been operated on in this manner.

Breakfast arrives just after six in the morning, I manage to get some orange juice, toast and marmalade and a bit of tea into me. My morning paper is delivered along with it but I barely have the concentration to watch television let alone read, perhaps I will get a chance later. Believe it or not, this tires me out and I slip back to sleep for a little while until my next 'obs' check arrives. Now that this is done and I am more awake, I make the decision that I

want to try and go to the toilet. I work myself to a
sitting position and swing my legs over the bed. I
carefully arrange all of the various tubes that surround
me until I am left with the urine drain attachment. I
pick up the drain as it's in a little wire basket and I
make my way around the bed slowly, one carefully
placed foot in front of the other, and reach the
connecting room that is my bathroom. This is the
first chance I have had to take a look at myself as
there is a mirror in there. I am shocked to see how
clammy and bloody I am. I feel dirty and decide to
use the shower which is in here. It's a wet room style
so it wasn't too much of a problem. My biggest issue
was removing the 'flight socks' so they didn't get wet.
I manage to do all that I had set out to do and more,
however it probably isn't my finest hour as I nearly
kill myself bending over for a period of time getting
those stockings off and then back on again. I manage
to get back to bed by the time Michelle comes in.
One look at me and she can see I am not right. When
I confess to her what I have been up to, I am in even
more pain and she goes ballistic!

"What were you thinking?"

"Where were the nurses?"

"Why didn't you buzz for them?"

"Why didn't you wait for me? I could have helped you."

"Fancy getting out of bed on your own like that, you have just had a major operation!"

"What are you like?"

She is livid with the nursing staff as no-one is checking up on me other than the two-hour observations. I tell her it's all done now; she disappears and returns with a nurse who looks at me like I am some kind of nut-ball and dispenses more lovely painkillers.

Once Michelle calms down, she gives me a smile that basically says, "you doughnut!" This morning hasn't gone well as the youngest daughter woke up full of cold and really groggy. This meant some drastic last-minute plans to get the oldest to her school which is a couple of miles away from where we live and someone in to look after our youngest while Michelle comes in to see me. I tell her she shouldn't have worried about coming in to see me. I can use this time to rest and catch up. We have a cup of coffee together and I persuade her to go home and sort our youngest out. If she still isn't well tonight don't panic, just let me or the nurses know, and we will catch up tomorrow. After a short time, she gives in and goes home, promising to return tonight if it's possible with the girls and some goodies.

Lunch comes and goes, I sleep a little, I watch a little TV, my 'obs' continue and generally I am not feeling too bad. The doctor looks in, examines me, asks me how I am feeling and tells me that all looks good. The plan is for me to return home tomorrow where I will need to rest for 6-8 weeks. In the first week or so, try to move around where possible to keep the blood flowing and reduce the chance of any blood clots. This is great news to me, I can't wait to tell Michelle and the girls later, hopefully. More sleep, what a life!

My youngest has made a miraculous recovery as only ten-year-olds can! I am thrilled to see them all and I can tell my appearance is a little more pleasing than the previous day. They have come with a picnic of really nice sandwiches, crisps, sausage rolls (my favourite) and tins of cold fizzy drink. Everyone agrees that I look so much better and they are overjoyed at the news that I am coming home tomorrow. I know immediately that Michelle thinks this is awful quick to be sending somebody home who has gone through what I have but she accepts it and knows that I am a tough cookie, and I would rather be home than anywhere else right now. We eat and chat, the girls lose focus on me and are drawn at some point to the television, while Michelle and I chat about me coming home. In no time at all it is time for them to leave. I thank them all for coming to see me, hugs, kisses and goodnight rituals played out and I mouth to Michelle "see you tomorrow" as one of the nurses comes in to do my 'obs', oh the dedication!

I am thrilled to be going home in the morning. I try to watch a little television, but I am not really in the mood. At some point I fall asleep; it's been a big day. Around midnight I am rudely awaken by a nurse for the regular 'obs'. I am a little slow in coming round as I am so knackered, that's the price your body pays for being dragged from your slumber every two hours. The nurse yanks me up from my rest position so violently I actually let out a scream in pain. I haven't had this nurse before and I am trying to explain to her how much discomfort I am in. She looks at me like I have come from another planet. I am trying to establish some sort of conversation with her but I genuinely believe she has no command of the English language and I seem to be wasting my time. She does the basics of what she came in to do, I ask for more pain relief and she seems to get my drift. She disappears and another nurse arrives. She can see I am in agony; she asks me if I have been given anything for the pain and I say no, she checks my chart and then dispenses some more tablets for the pain, scribbles this onto my record and leaves me to pass out.

At some point I wake; I can tell it's early morning because there is a small amount of light coming into the room from the window to the left of me. I am immediately hit by a searing pain in my stomach and for the first time, I squeeze my 'panic button'. I am sure I can hear people moving around just outside my door in the corridor but even though the light is on from me pushing the button and it also emits a loud buzzer noise, nobody comes. I press it again and again; I am in agony. Nothing! I force myself up into a sitting position, clamber out of bed and retrieve my urine bag, which is still attached. I make my way out of my room and look desperately up and down the corridor, bizarrely there is no-one to be seen. I clamber over to the nurses' station and they look at me in complete shock. I explain in no uncertain terms that I am in bloody agony and I am less than happy as I have been pressing their sodding button and no-one has responded. They usher me back to bed and sort out some further medication and go back to checking me every twenty minutes. Back to sleep.

As morning arrives fully, breakfast is served and consumed as I seem to have an appetite today. Shortly after this one of the doctors arrives. He greets me with a hardy, "Good morning," and continues to pepper me with questions while he takes my pulse and gives the chart at the end of my bed the once over. He does a quick examination and appears happy with everything. I tell him about the pain I had been in and he explains that this is not unusual given the circumstances. He is going to organise my meds and my release form so I can go home later this morning and he will organise a nurse to swing by with instructions for what meds to take and when. He beckons one of the nurses in and supervises while the urine drain that is attached to me is removed.

I text Michelle the news that I am definitely coming home this morning. I start getting myself ready and carefully, wash, dress and organise my things. Michelle arrives and finishes packing for me. At this point we sit and wait with the BBC News on in the background as this is all we can do until they tell us we can go. About 30 minutes later a nurse pops in and empties out the contents of a large bag she has brought with her. She explains more to Michelle than me about which pills are which, when to take them and how many. It's all printed on the boxes to help. She then gets out fresh dressings for me to change every 2 days for the next 10 days. At this point she waves a clear bag with what looks like a pair of wire cutters inside. We are told to book an appointment at our local surgery for one of the nurses to remove the clips in my wound and that was it. Any issues, contact your local doctors and with that you are free to go. We both thank her at once, Michelle grabs my bag with one arm and me with the other, helps me out of the room and left along the corridor to the lift that goes all of the way down to the car park level. I shuffle along like a little old man expressing my goodbyes to everyone I pass. Michelle organises me into a chair at the rear end reception and says she will bring the car around. Getting in the car was a bit of a palaver, sorting out a comfortable position for the seat belt was even more so. With no malice whatsoever towards my wife's driving skills, I can honestly tell you I felt every bump and pothole in the road on my journey home. As we are driving, we chat and it's clear Michelle is happy that I am still here and she has organised things at home to make my rest period as easy for me as possible. She tells me that lots of people have been enquiring about me and want to visit but I say I am not quite up to that yet but it's kind that they are thinking of me.

Home. Greeted by our chocolate Labrador who is clearly pleased to see me. Michelle guides me inside, settles me into a comfy leather armchair which is right in front of our forty-inch television and hands me the Sky remote – bliss! Shortly afterwards, tea and apple cream turnovers arrive, blooming heck, I should have cancer more often!

The girls rush home from school and both fuss over me for at least 10 minutes before disappearing with the leftover cakes. Kids being kids, within just a couple of days they have forgotten all about how ill I had been and were like, "Dad, where's this?" "Dad, I can't find so and so." Talk about back to normal! My brother was the first person I wanted to see. He was desperate to come into the hospital and see me, but I did not want to make a big thing out of it and told him to come and see me when I was feeling better and we could talk more. It was great to see him, although we only live fifteen minutes apart, we do not see a huge amount of one another. He is 7 years older than me, got married before me, had his two children way before me, works permanent nights and our paths do not cross as often as we would both like. We have always done boys weekends away with some of the guys from our local pub and joint friends and we go to Newbury every September for the horse racing. This is something we used to do every year with our old fella, he loved his horses and loved to gamble on them. He never bet on anything else, just the horses. My brother and I have been going to Newbury for over 40 years, missing only about three occasions, for various reasons, in all that time. He is clearly pleased to see me and admires the relatively good state I appear to be in. It's great to see him, he is my only blood relative outside of my daughters, as both our parents are long gone. I believe there is the odd aunt, uncle and a few cousins knocking about still but I haven't seen any of these people in years, probably not since Mum passed away early 2010. He asks me about my time in hospital and what happens next. I explain all that has happened and that once the clips get removed the following week at the doctors surgery, I have to wait on a letter from Urology to have another CT scan in about three months and then the consultant will meet with me to discuss the results. We discuss work, our families and some of our friends over a coffee and he takes his leave when he can see I am starting to tire.

Over the next couple of weeks, I can honestly say I spent at least half of my time in bed, sometimes for 2 or 3 days on the trot. Tired doesn't even begin to describe it! It is total fatigue. Never have I felt so knackered in all my life. When it comes over you, all you can think of is crawling into bed and closing your eyes, you don't sit up, watch TV or read, you haven't even got the strength to get up to go to the loo, it's totally debilitating.

Friends phone and text to see how I am, am I up for a visit? The enquiries are very kind but Michelle fends off most of them as on the whole I am just not up to it. I manage to see a few people, but it is not long before I must make my excuses and disappear back to bed. It is a bit of a surreal experience because once I finish the painkillers, that is it. There is no further medication, no chemotherapy or radiotherapy like my dad had to have after his operation, nothing. Again I feel a bit of a fraud!

The day comes for the clips to be removed. Michelle drives me the couple of minutes it takes to get to our doctors surgery. We book in and take a couple of seats in the large waiting room. Within no time the nurse comes out, smiles at us, and calls out my name. I identify myself, introduce Michelle and we both get invited into her room. We chat about what has been going on with me. Michelle hands her the surgical bag with the wire cutters whilst the nurse checks her computer for the notes. Once she is happy, I remove my t-shirt and she strips off the latest dressing. The whole of my right side is quite red and itchy and although I do suffer with some psoriasis, it appears to be a reaction to the plastic-based dressing (after a day or so it would be gone). She decides to continue after we discuss it and with a few loud clunks, the clips are removed. A new different dressing is offered but I decline, there is no bleeding so let's just let the fresh air help it heal. After a few more pleasantries we are free to go and that is it. All I can do now is rest, get strong and look forward to Disney World, Florida with Michelle and the kids.

Oddly, in the time that passes I begin to feel like I have something missing. I do not know if it is because I am at home resting while everyone else is going about their day, but the lack of normality is starting to have an effect on me. It's the little things that are beginning to grate. Not seeing the boys at work and having the craic, going for a pint afterwards and meeting up with some of the other guys we know in the trade, swapping insults and comparing stories. The consultant tells me that I am no longer to do any contact sports, well, up until the week before my operation I was still playing five-a-side football (I know, at my age?). I have played eleven-a-side and five-a-side football since I could kick a ball! I did give it up for a short while when in my early thirties, but I missed playing so much it made me miserable and some of the young lads I was working with at the time lassoed me in to playing with them. It was great to be back and although all the younger ones could run rings around me, I could still hold my own. Actually, let me tell you this: there is not a time in my life that I can remember not being associated with a football team, however I am the only guy in the whole of the UK who has played for almost fifty years for various teams and has never had a trial for anybody! Truth being, I was never that good, always enthusiastic, at times not bad (every dog has his day!) but truly never great. Now, as I don't have the strength to exercise, I feel physically weak and to make matters worse, for some reason I have started crying at the sad parts in films and we are not talking about Bambi's mum having her head blown off by a shotgun. Even some of the adverts are setting me off, what the hell is going on?

It's now coming up to July, the summer so far has been kind and I have been dragging myself out of bed in the late morning and crashing in the back garden. I have a decent tan and I am looking forward to our upcoming holiday. Michelle has voiced her concerns several times to me about whether I am fit enough for a 10 hour flight and then all of the activities we will be attempting, it's not like crashing on a beach for two weeks, but I assure her I will be fine. In fact, I tell her I am going if it bloody well kills me, and she says this is what she is worried about! I decide to go back to work, I need to get back to some sort of routine as I am just not used to this quiet, relaxed life. I have worked every day since I left school at sixteen apart from a couple of months when I was once made redundant. After talking it through with my doctor and approaching my boss at work, it is decided that I will return on what they call a 'phased return to work' starting at 15 hours a week. I am given a doctors note that reflects this, dated for a month, and I make my return. To start with I just do a couple of hours every other day. Everyone is very kind and seems happy to see me. To be fair, I do find it quite hard to start with and I do miss a few days where I am bedridden again with fatigue (something that I still get from time to time even now, over six years later at the time of writing this). What is really nice is that my oldest daughter, although still at school, works part-time on a Saturday as the sales receptionist and she was amazed at how many of my customers rang up just to enquire how I was doing. Once word gets out that I am back, I have lots of previous customers coming in for a chat, some introducing family or friends for me to deal with. Others, particularly the older ones, come in for a chat and free cup of coffee. Brilliant. Funny story, typical car salesperson. When I left the business for my operation, we were already one person short.

They recruited a couple of guys; one I still have the pleasure of working with now and the other a complete shyster (every car dealership has at least one!). So, I pop out on a test drive with a new customer and when I return about 20 minutes later, I escort the customer to my desk with a nice hot drink and return to the car we have just driven to put it back on the lot. We are not blessed with a lot of customer parking so it's something we all (well, most of us!) do. As I walk back into the showroom, I am aware there is a lady walking in behind me so I stop, hold the door open for her and greet her with, "Hello, can I help you at all?" She lets out an almighty shriek and blurts out, "They told me you were dead!" It turns out she had phoned in, got through to the salesroom and got one of the new sales guys (yep, you guessed it, the shyster), she explained her car was 3 years old and wanted to part exchange it for a new one, she then asked for me as I had sold her the car and stated that I had made the whole transaction very enjoyable. At this point she was given the sad news of my demise and invited in by this ever so caring individual who made a few bob out of my customer's suffering and my apparent demise, what a lovely chap! True story. That's car sales for you!

After 4 weeks of this interrupted work pattern, we take off on holiday for 2 weeks. Michelle made sure I had my flight socks on for the flight and scowled at me every now and again which meant pause the film and go for a little walk even though I am 5 miles up in the air. The flight was fine, to be fair it was far from a relaxing holiday, but it was one of the best ones I have ever been on. So much to see and do, great weather, fantastic service, and the staff, wherever you go in Florida, are so welcoming and courteous, I would definitely go again. Apart from one morning where I was not feeling up to it, Michelle and the girls had a morning by the pool while I just caught up, I managed to get through the whole holiday. It truly was magic.

Back to reality, it's late August 2015, and I'm back to work full-time now. While we were away a letter dropped onto the mat inviting me for a CT scan at Southmead hospital. This was to be my first follow-up since the operation. This time I persuaded

Michelle there was no need for her to come as she could only sit and wait while I go in and get it done. There is no immediate conclusion, and we will soon find out when we see the consultant. The next couple of weeks really drag for all of us as the girls are aware of the situation. We made the decision to keep it light and not scare them about it but to keep them involved in the process so that should the worse come into play, it won't be as much of a shock. We get a letter and a date to see the consultant and we duly attend. We are greeted like old friends and guided into a different room this time. He gives me a quick examination and asks me how I am doing. He has my latest scan on a large flat screen in front of him and expertly guides us through the different sections of my upper body. All good, no sign of any cancer, he is really happy with the way everything has gone. He discusses the histology report (the results of the dissection of my kidney and its cancerous cells) and confirms it is exactly as he thought. He goes on to say that this type of cancer is extremely rare in someone of my age, normally they would only see this in a much older person or somebody who was clinically obese (hey, I am six foot three and around fourteen stone with a near perfect body index, thank you very much!). He then goes on to say that because of this there is a one in two chance that it may, not definitely but may, return! My brain doesn't compute this at first. Michelle asks a few questions, I think, I am in partial shutdown. I am going to be placed in 'remission' (this is where they continue to check on you, normally annually) for the next 10 years. I would have another CT scan in 6 months, followed up with a consultant meeting, then it was planned for once a year until my 10 years was done. We leave more than a little deflated but once in the car we decide sod it, you only live once, I am clear and fine right now, let's just get on with it, and get on with it we did. By the end of the week we had 2 weeks holiday booked for the following summer in Cancun, Mexico – yeeha muchachos!

For me, things go on as close to normal as possible, I have a new normal now. Because I am still having the occasional days off work through the fatigue, I manage to get the company to look at changing my contract slightly. I still work similar hours to all of the other guys, but I now work Monday to Friday and every other Sunday whereas before I had Tuesdays off and every other Sunday. The hours can be brutal in the car trade. Every now and then Michelle would want to talk about it, it upsets her to know that I am carrying this burden around with me and doing my best not to show it to anyone. She is concerned about the girls not having me around and how unfair it all is. I do my best to reassure her I will be fine. I am made of tough stuff; I am a Collins! Things continue along as they always do, night follows day, and we settle into our new slightly scary routine.

Christmas and New Year come and go. It's toward the anniversary of all this starting when another letter drops through the letterbox and it's time for yet another CT scan. The 6 months since the last one seems like an eternity and now here we go again, it is pushed from the back of our thoughts to the forefront once again. In the lead up to the scan we are both a little twitchy and careful not to discuss it too much. Again, I attend the scan on my own, number three in less than a year (I have just completed number twelve today as I'm writing this, what a coincidence). The wait is on for the consultant letter. It comes the following week with an appointment booked for a fortnight's time. This time it is a much younger doctor who comes out to greet us. He introduces himself and explains that my case notes have been passed on to him. He sits us down and shows us the latest scan. It's all good news, all clear. He checks my scarring and asks if I have any questions. We are careful with the words we use but we both quiz him a little more on this one in two chance of it coming back. Obviously, it is the sixty-four-million-dollar question and he is wary of giving an answer mainly because he can't. He tells us that with the evidence that he has seen in my case, I should make the most of every day. That told us what we really didn't want to hear but we definitely needed to hear. Michelle was really upset when we came away from the consultation. I could only put my arms around her and tell her not to worry, I am all good at the moment, they are looking for it yearly and if something happens, we will deal with it then. We have the girls to think about and that has always been our priority, to protect them, they are still so young to have to be dealing with all this. I am determined it is not going to have me yet and so, from early 2016, that is how we proceed. We carry on with life as normal, work, play, socialise, and just get on with it. Michelle and I talk about it from time to time, it's always her that starts the conversation. I am not saying I have not had the odd dark day, because I have. I can tell you one thing though and as bullish as this sounds, it is not meant to: I am not afraid to die. It's the only thing you can guarantee in life. I just don't want to go yet, I have too many things I still want to see and do.

Funny how life just continues, you see disasters on the news, people going through the most horrible of things, people you know having their own personal issues, deaths in the family and amongst friends but tomorrow still comes just the same. That is how it is for us; we are all getting on with it because what else are we supposed to do? We enter 2017, it's scan time again. It's been a year now, I am not aware of any issues, haven't been anywhere near a doctor or a hospital and I am back playing five-a-side football, sod 'em. Once again, I attend Southmead Hospital on my own, same routine. We wait for the letter to arrive for the follow up appointment. It doesn't! It's been over two weeks since my last scan and there is no appointment sent through. I hit the phones, at first I seem to be passed from one person to another before I get my original consultant's secretary. She is very apologetic about my not being contacted, she explains very carefully that there have been some unexpected changes within the Urology department, and they are doing their best to catch up. She realises and completely understands that I am anxious to know the results of my scan and promises to get one of the consulting team to call me and explain the latest news to me over the phone if I am happy to do it that way. I assure her that I am, and she takes my mobile number so that this can happen. I get the call the next day. It's short and sweet, all good for now, all clear, any issues give us a call, apologies once again. At this point we are both relieved, we tell the girls and celebrate by booking our next summer holiday in the Dominican Republic – can't wait. Holidays abroad are massive in our house, both Michelle and I love to travel, something we have been lucky enough to do quite extensively in the almost thirty years we have now been together. Both the girls have also inherited this desire to see other countries and embrace their cultures. Due to the yearly check to see if I am going to be around, we do not tempt fate, we only book once I have the all-clear.

It turns out that all of this upheaval waiting for my results was caused by my original consultant, the very top man in this field, the man who operated on me and I owe my life to, having a similar cancer found on his kidney. He needed a similar operation to remove the cancer but unfortunately his heart wasn't strong enough and it gave out on him on the operating table, there was nothing any of his team could do. We had both just turned fifty, a real milestone for me as at one point I did not necessarily think I would get that far. Ultimately he saved me and could not be saved himself, how bloody ironic is that? Life can be so cruel. We were so shocked.

A month or so later Michelle contacted the Urology team at Southmead and asks if she can do a fundraiser in honour and appreciation of what had been done for me. We were not the only ones devastated by his passing. One of my best friends of over 40 years also had him as his lead consultant when he was diagnosed and treated for prostate cancer a couple of years before. Michelle swings into high gear, she does a coffee and cake morning at our house which goes on all day. My boss and I even manage to attend for half an hour, I've never seen so many people in our house all at once. This is followed by an evening at our local curry house. Almost thirty people attend, we have drinks, a fantastic meal, Michelle organised a raffle and managed to scrounge up all sorts of prizes. The restaurant give a donation as well and apart from me embarrassing myself with a slightly drunken speech, a good night is had by all and we/Michelle raised almost eight hundred pounds which is passed along to the appropriate benefactors.

The whole event shakes us out of our comfort zone a little. I notice that there seems to be more occasions where we discuss it. Maybe it's because the girls are a little older, more independent, out doing stuff with their friends and we are left with more time to ourselves, who knows? I think at this time, I resigned myself to the fact that this awful, shitty disease will more than likely be the end of me but brother, we've got a way to go yet! I have no intention of giving in to it.

The year passes, early 2018 brings my annual CT scan and it's same old, same old. All clear, just carry on as normal. We plan our summer holiday; this time we are off to Thailand, the 'land of smiles'. Michelle and I have been there before, although we are going to different parts this time, the girls will love it. There are other projects we are thinking about and plan a celebration of our twenty-fifth wedding anniversary. We continue to try and enjoy life as best we can. We have always done our best to not let it take over our lives, it's something that we are all conscious of, but we just continue with what we are doing and that's fine with me. Life still goes on.

THE SECOND JOURNEY

2019 sees my eldest daughter settling into full-time employment, my youngest about to start her final year in secondary school and looking at taking her GCSEs before hopefully going onto college, and my fourth yearly CT scan. Once again, I attend Southmead Hospital, I know the routine so well by now I could tell the staff what needed doing. To be fair I was a bit blasé about it. I felt good, so good that this year's family holiday is already booked for early August, Jamaica this time. I'm looking forward to it, still playing football, relatively fit, just turned fifty-two. It's been 4 years now since all this started, life seems good, surely, I must be in the clear.

The follow-up letter states that I will be contacted by phone with the results of my latest scan by one of the specialist nursing team. I remember clearly, it's a Thursday morning, ten a.m. and my mobile rings. I put it on speaker phone, confirm my name and say, "Good morning," and explain that Michelle is here with me as well. More pleasantries and once the introductions are made, she gets down to business. "Not good news I am afraid." We look at one another and our hearts sink. "The cancer is back, this time it is in your chest. The scan shows a 1-centimetre cancerous lymph nodule and we will need to remove it as soon as we can. I am passing all of your details over to the Cardiothoracic team and they will be in touch shortly."

We do our best to hide our disappointment. She goes on to say that this is thought to be in keeping with the original renal cell carcinoma. Sorry to be the bearer of such bad news, if we have any further questions, just call. She hangs up after we thank her for her call. Michelle is in bits; my mind is racing and we console each other. After a few minutes we get ourselves together, grab a coffee and sit and talk about it. We decide to tell the girls straight away and prepare them for me to go in for a second stage three operation. Later that afternoon, when we are all sat down together, we tell them the results of the scan. They are shocked, a few tears arrive and as usual I go into, "Come on, it will all be alright, they found it early, I've done it once and I can do it again," mode. They both hug me and fight to control their emotions. Michelle's eyes are moist, I think even the bloody dog is crying!

Very soon after I receive a letter from the Cardiothoracic department inviting me to see one of their consultants. Here we go again!

This time the operation is to be in the BRI (Bristol Royal Infirmary) and once again, Michelle is with me as we are asked to go back to Southmead Hospital in the first instance to go through the preliminaries. We are met by one of the specialist cancer nurses and she runs us through what is going to happen today. I have my temperature checked, blood pressure taken, weight recorded and some bloods taken just for good measure. I then get sent off for a chest x-ray. Once that is done, we go for something to eat as we are asked to kill some time so that my new consultant can look at the x-ray, the previous month's scan and the results of the tests they have taken this morning.

We return to where we started and don't have to wait very long before we are invited in to meet the new consultant and the specialist cancer nurse from earlier sits in with us. Introductions done, the consultant asks some background questions to start with and then goes through my last scan and compares it to my latest chest x-ray. The lymph node has grown to 2.4 centimetres and the decision is made to operate as soon as possible. She points out that I am still relatively young, fit and strong and that this is the only option. We all agree on this and they arrange for me to come back early the following week to have some lung function tests. At this point we are asked to go away for a coffee while they try and set up a zoom call with the Cardiothoracic team based at the BRI as that's who will be performing the operation. They will need to talk to me about the operation and will want to ask me some questions before arranging the pre-op and then proceed to the operation.

An hour later we are beckoned into a small office, there is a computer screen with a menu loaded on it, webcam attached with a microphone and a set of speakers. We are told to sit and wait until the screen changes and alerts us of an incoming call and we will be face to face with the surgeon, theatre nurse, anaesthetist, and the ward practise manager. They are all making time in their already busy day to talk to us and this is thought to be a better idea than us driving there and trying to catch all of these people. This great idea is in fact a nightmare! The first time a call comes in there is no sound so we can't hear what is being asked or said. Then the Wi-Fi bombs out. Then, when it comes back on, the first person we are talking to has been called away. So, we sit looking at an empty office in the BRI while we wait for someone to come in. Eventually we do manage to speak to all of them individually and work out all of the requirements so they can organise not only the pre-op that is needed but also the date of the operation itself.

I am upbeat about it, let's just get it done and get on with life. I know Michelle appreciates my efforts at being positive and we carry this on when we tell the girls. I am dreading telling my brother and my best friends that I have it again. They are all devastated to hear our news but rally round with offers of any help needed and support if I or we need anyone to talk to. Michelle lets everybody else know and we are inundated with offers of help and best wishes. I have to tell my boss (different chap to my first occasion and I still work for him now), he was great about it, told me not to worry, the company would look after me and just do whatever you need to do.

The following Monday I leave work at around five p.m. and head towards North Bristol which is where Southmead hospital is based, it takes me forty minutes as it is just entering 'rush hour'. My appointment is at six and by the time I get parked and book in, I just make it to the appropriate department as they call me in. The nurse who called me introduces herself and beckons me to follow her through a maze of corridors that eventually lead to a small room. Once in she sits me down and goes through the normal question routine. She asks me to take a seat in an apparatus at the back of the room that looks a little like an old-fashioned phone box without the glass panes. I do as requested and she unwraps a plastic mouthpiece and explains how to fit it to the large plastic air filter that is now directly in front of my face. The chair I am on is like one of those windy stools you get in photo booths. I adjust it accordingly and once prompted follow the instructions given for holding breath and expelling it for the times that I am told. This procedure is repeated several times and once over, she explains that they would put a rush on the results which would be passed to the consultant to see if I was fit for surgery. This would be at least a couple of days. I drive home and tell my little audience all that has happened.

I get a call three days later asking me to come in to the BRI the following Tuesday for my pre-op. I find some quiet time over the weekend and decide to write out my funeral details, just in case. I am positive I will survive this surgery but need to put my ducks in a row as this disease is getting another chance to bite me. I put together a little eulogy that I would like read, make a list of the music I want played and ask that no hymns or psalms are done. I am happy to have the Lord's Prayer as I believe this to be respectful but no other religious elements. I leave details of where I wish the service to be and I leave it up to Michelle whether she wants me barbecued or buried. I manage to put some private letters together for not only Michelle and the girls but my brother, my closest friends and those that are close to us as a family.

On the Monday morning, my boss lets me explain to the team that my cancer has returned. I am going to be out of the business this time for around 3 months and I need to select someone to help out delivering almost forty cars to onward waiting customers. This time it overwhelms me and I cry whilst sharing this news with them. There are other wet eyes in the room and somebody eventually pipes up with something humorous and we all break into a laugh.

Michelle comes with me for the pre-op which is the usual procedure: ECG, bloods, temperature, blood pressure and blood sugar tests, although this didn't quite go as planned. When they took my bloods they didn't take the correct amount and then because they had already closed off where they had inserted the cannula they had to then put a new one in my other arm. Then, bless her, the nurse could not get the ECG machine to work and there was a comedy moment where I think even she had no idea what she was doing, holding a handful of cables and trying to work out what went where. I am not sure if it was by design or just luck that she managed to get it to work in the end. Pre-op shakes dispensed with, we're given the printed letter that explains the do's and don'ts before coming in for the operation and the time and date, June fourteenth, seven a.m., BRI level six.

I bid my colleagues farewell on the Thursday evening and head for home. The girls are both in and after a quick dog walk, we order a Chinese takeaway and tuck into a feast of egg fried rice, sticky chilli beef, chicken chow mein, and prawn crackers with a side of chips and curry sauce – what a last meal! We crash out on the sofa, take in a film and share some chocolate, my kind of family evening. As the night draws to an end, I get a cuddle from both of them, exchange "love you's" and we say goodnight, "See you guys tomorrow."

Morning comes, Friday, fourteenth of June, 2019. No need for any sitters as the girls are old enough to sort themselves out. Once Michelle has ticked off her 'check list' we are ready to go. My oldest daughter drives us in to the hospital, as she works in the centre of Bristol she has kindly volunteered to take us in for the seven o' clock start and then head on into work a little earlier as she normally starts at eight. She drops us right outside the main reception and kisses us both goodbye after agreeing with Michelle that when she finishes work at one, she will double back and get her sister who we have understandably let have the day off. She promises to return with her as soon as she can which will be around two. We make our way into the main reception and find the lifts. We head up to level six and report to the pre-op department for the second time in less than a fortnight. The nurses smile, tick me off their list and guide us to a little changing room. We are told we can wait here; someone will be with us shortly. A nurse arrives with a list, checks me off and passes me two wristbands complete with my name, date of birth and hospital number on. Once fitted she asks me if I have had anything to eat or drink in the last two hours other than the pre-op drinks I was dispensed with. Once all of her questions are answered she tells me the anaesthetist will be along shortly. When I am ready, could I please put on the gown provided and then she makes a list of all of the items I have brought in with me for my stay. She then hands Michelle a tag to connect to my overnight bag. The porter will collect it at the same time he comes for me. We ask about what time I will be going down to theatre and she says there are a couple in front of me so probably sometime around ten.

The anaesthetist comes by for a quick chat, more questions, identity checked and what do I think I am in for. All good, quick examination and explanation to both of us, they hope they can just 'slip' the cancerous cell off as it has attached itself to one of my arteries, hopefully it will only be an hour or so. Sounds good. See you down there and he is gone. We nervously chatter, Michelle is desperate for a coffee but won't leave me in case they come for me while she is gone. In no time at all a jolly type of chap turns up with a wheelchair and asks me if I want to ride or walk. I opt to walk and he grabs my bag. We only go fifty metres or so, he announces this is as far as Michelle can go, we hug and kiss, utter "I love you" to each other and as I disappear through the double doors I say, "See you later," Once through the doors the porter hands me over to the anaesthetist and some of the assembled team. They ask me to hop up on the bed that is in front of me and start asking me the same old questions that cover my identity and why I am there. Again, they go through the basics of what is happening and I have a couple of cannulas put in. They explain briefly what they are for, one last check on my identity tags and I get a question about why I have the Everton Football Club badge tattooed on my upper right arm. I explain it's a long story but they have been my side since I was a little boy and then I get the count back from ten command. Ten, nine, eigh…

At this point again I will hand the reins over to Michelle to explain what happened while I was doing my Sleeping Beauty act!

I can't believe we are at this junction again. It seems surreal after almost 4 years of pretty much perfect health that he is here again. It seems so unfair, not just on him but on the girls as well. I feel awful that there is nothing I can do to help him, like a guilty feeling that somehow I could have stopped it. Unlike his last operation, where he was taken from his own room, here all of the people booked in for an operation on any given day all get collected from this central area so there is no point in me staying here but they have said to check back later to find out what ward he will be taken to once out of the operating theatre. I wander off down to the main reception, get a Costa and sit trying to concentrate on the free Bristol Metro newspapers that are strewn everywhere. It doesn't take long before I lose interest in this and decide, as I am only a ten minute or less walk away from the main Bristol Broadmead shopping area, that I will go and have a wander as it will kill some time.

I cross over the main road that runs parallel with the hospital and head south, walking towards the bus station. Over another really busy road and I am there. I normally love to browse and shop, given the time, but I don't actually remember where I went or if I purchased anything but I do remember the rain. The heavens opened and it hammered down, catching most people out as it was a relatively nice summers day. I head back up the hill towards the hospital and return to level six. They report that he is still in theatre and so I wander back down to the main reception. It's taking longer than they originally intended so I am worried about what's happening. It's now after twelve. I decide to grab a sandwich and a cold drink from Marks and Spencer and text both of the girls. They are both sorted for lunch and will be here in an hour or so. I leave it for a bit then I go back up to level six. They inform me that he had been taken to recovery. Great, he has made it off the table again, hopefully I will see him soon. I am back in reception when the girls arrive. I buy them their favourite coffees and explain that dad went into the recovery ward about an hour ago. We all head up to level six expecting to then be directed to which ward they have put him on. Back at the level six reception desk, I get the feeling that they are fed up with seeing me. I enquire as to where they have sent him. You know when you get that feeling you're not getting the whole story? Well, that's how I am feeling at this moment. There's a long pause, some long staring at the computer screen and then another member of staff looks into it. "He is still in recovery, I am afraid," comes the answer. Her colleague takes over and calls *the recovery unit. After a few moments I get the offer of going down to the recovery ward to see him, if I would like to. It turns out he is struggling with his body temperature and they are trying to get enough warmth into his body for him to come around properly from the op. On the outside I am nodding that I understand but inside I am freaking out. The girls both have a worried look across their faces and we are told only one person can go onto the resus ward. I can see the girls are starting to get upset, I reassure them and say to them to sit here while I go and check on Dad. My mind is racing, I am not sure what I am about to come across, I have to wait for somebody to accompany me down to Resus so we are all just sitting, worrying and trying to keep it all together. I will be brutally honest here, I was mentally preparing myself for the worst but I knew with the girls here in front of me I had to dig deep and get on with it. Never has time ever passed as slow, it was only about 10 minutes and just as someone turned up to escort me, blow me, he gets wheeled past us, forces a little smile and a thumbs up and has a large silver foil blanket wrapped around him – he looks like a bad seventies disco singer! We follow the bed as they take him along to the ward. We are asked to give them five minutes to settle him in and originally they took him into room six. For some reason, when we are allowed to follow, they have*

moved him into room twelve but we find him in the end.
Relieved he is back with us, we fuss around him for a little bit
and then, realising just how tired he is, we leave him to rest,
promising to return in a couple of hours.

I remember someone softly calling my name. There it is again, it's definitely a woman's voice but not Michelle. I struggle to open my eyes; the room is dark with soft lighting coming from the other side of a large room. As I try to focus, I see the footers of other hospital beds opposite me. The woman's voice is now backed up by a partial sighting of her face as she has a mask on over her mouth. She leans in towards me and says, "Hello, can you tell me your name?" I do my best to convey who I am, my throat is incredibly sore and my voice is raspy. She tells me that I am on the Resus ward and I will be moved up to another ward in a little while. At this point I pass back out, not sure if I have just dreamt this or not.

I vaguely remember passing Michelle and the girls whilst flat out on my bed. I force a smile and give a little wave at them to indicate I am still alive. Once I am parked and hooked up to various gadgets, including a chest drain, Michelle and the girls are allowed in. They are more than pleased to see me, I get the impression that they have been waiting longer perhaps than they were expecting and the shared relief between them is palpable. I am wrapped in one of those big foil sheets, the ones you see getting wrapped around marathon runners on completion of their race. Again, I am lucky enough to have my own room with a TV and my own bathroom. After a few minutes, they make the decision to leave and let me rest, they can see that I am all in at the moment and promise to return in the evening. At this stage I am completely unaware of what time it is. It is late afternoon; the surgery took longer than anticipated and for some reason it took a lot longer for me to come back around once the op was done. They could not get my body temperature to rise hence the Christmas turkey look.

Michelle and the girls go to the nearest Nando's, which is about half a mile away, for dinner. They drag it out for a couple of hours and return to check on me, staying for a little while. They all fuss over me but realise I am still really groggy and leave, promising to return tomorrow. The foil has gone and I am wrapped up in a sheet and blankets. I have a pipe coming out of the left side of my chest, it's relatively uncomfortable and it was explained to me that this would need to stay in only while I am in hospital. It goes right down into the bottom of my stomach and it takes me a while to find a suitable position to either sit up or lay down. During all of this time I am on thirty-minute obs – boy have I missed this! I manage to squeeze in some sleep which is really down to the pills they are pumping into me. The obs continue into the night and the length of time changes to every hour so I manage a bit more rest.

I'm not sure why but I have woken, there's no one in my room or in the corridor alongside and it's deathly quiet. As my eyes begin to adjust to the dark my breathing starts to go completely out of rhythm. I can't catch my breath and the more I try to understand what's happening, the worse it's getting. I try to gather my thoughts but my chest is racing up and down and I am shaking. I manage to squeeze the 'panic button'. Almost immediately a nurse arrives and can clearly see I am in some distress, I try to explain but I can't breathe! He disappears just for a moment and on his return tells me to try and relax, he snaps a small portable style hypodermic needle and injects me in the bottom of my stomach with a small dose of morphine. My body goes into a relaxed state almost immediately and after a few more words of comfort, I slump back to sleep.

Morning comes at last, it's an early breakfast here, just after six. More obs, more pills, the usual painkillers and laxatives – need to get those bowels moving! Two young doctors arrive. They look at my charts, we discuss how the night went and one of them gives me a quick examination. They seem satisfied, tell me to rest up and they will pop back later this afternoon. I watch a bit of BBC News, drift off back to sleep for a little while and later in the morning I receive a light bed bath. The nurses encourage me to try and get out of bed to get my circulation going and, of course, there is a need to be able to go to the toilet, both ends, as otherwise I will not be allowed home.

I have no recollection whatsoever of lunch but I

do remember the Greggs sausage rolls Michelle and the girls arrived with (I do love their sausage rolls). We have a proper catch up, Michelle goes through all of the events of yesterday and I recap last night's almost 'panic attack'. I also tell her, away from the girls who have now disappeared to one of the Costas that are based here in the hospital main reception, about a conversation that I overheard between two nurses outside of my door last night. I could hear some chatting coming from the corridor, my room door was open and some light was filtering through. In hushed tones I could hear a woman's voice saying, "This one was touch and go apparently, nicked into his artery and they lost him for a bit." Michelle was visibly shocked; we ask the doctors about this later but are told they were not aware of any such issues. The nurse pops by, checks my obs and has a little chat with us both saying that all is going well, it's good that I have got out of bed and walked around a little. Just need to get the being able to go to the toilet both ends sorted and I should be able to go home. The girls return, it's so nice to see their independence. The oldest one is now eighteen and the younger one is coming up to fifteen, they are both more like young ladies rather than girls. We chat for a while about all that is going on, I assure them I am ok, will hopefully be home tomorrow if possible and all steam ahead for our Caribbean holiday in 10 weeks' time. It's late in the afternoon so I encourage them to go home, it's a Saturday night for goodness sake, go and enjoy yourselves, I will be fine. Call me in the morning. After kisses and hugs they all shuffle out and I try and doze for a bit.

The obs are now every two hours so I am getting more rest. I am not suffering any real pain and I am more alert and much more awake. Dinner comes and goes and as promised, the two young lady doctors I saw earlier return. They look at my chart and do a quick examination and they're gone. I watch some early evening TV, what a load of garbage all the terrestrial stations put on, to think you have to pay a TV licence for some of that tosh! I use this as inspiration to make myself go to the toilet. I head to my adjoining bathroom with my chest drain in tow. I try everything but nothing is happening. I am not sure how long I was in there but eventually, with the aid of the taps running, I manage to squeeze out a few drops from the front end. It's a start. I literally crawl back to bed – that was exhausting. After more obs I crash for a bit more sleep.

It's all dark and quiet, it must be around midnight. I wait for my latest round of obs and then quietly remove myself in stealth mode back to the bathroom. I am determined to be able to use the toilet so I might be able to go home tomorrow. I have no idea of time; it feels like I have been in here for hours. I am able to urinate without any issue now but I am continuing to struggle with the rear end. I am huffing and puffing, red in the face and doubled up bent at the waist incurring some pain but I have to make this happen. At last, success. I'm knackered but happy and make my way back to bed.

The routine continues, breakfast is consumed and I am looking forward to the doctors round, hopefully I can get out of here today. Different doctor this morning, must be a shift change. He studies my notes, asks me how I am feeling, says I have made a good recovery and I ask him if I can go home. I assure him I have dealt with the 'ablutions' issue and he says he will be back after his rounds and he will see what he can organise. I call home and tell Michelle the good news. It's still early but Michelle says she will be in with the girls around eleven. The doctor returns, sorts out my release form and tells me that I will need to have my chest drain removed, he will get one of the nurses in to do this. I will need to have a final chest x-Ray before I go and he will contact the hospital pharmacy and get all of the drugs I need to use organised and delivered to me here before I can then go.

Michelle and the girls arrive pretty much on time. I explain what is happening and that I am just waiting now. After 20 minutes or so the girls are bored and go on a walkabout. Michelle and I are chatting when two nurses arrive. They are here to remove my chest drain. Michelle asks if they want her to leave and they tell her no, it's fine. I drop off my gown on the left side, one of them tells me to breathe in, then wallop, she just yanks it out! There's no science to it, bloody hell did that hurt! It was like the worst 'carpet burn' you can ever experience. Quick mop up of the area, a couple of dissolvable stitches and done. Stage one complete. Another hour passes before a porter arrives with a wheelchair to take me for an x-ray. Once I am loaded in, off we go. It takes about ten minutes to get there, I am now in a queue. There are a couple of others waiting and I just sit there with nothing else to do until it is my time. It's now after two, unknown to me at this time the girls have gone off and topped up the parking as the car is on a metre, as I led them to believe we would be going home later that morning. They raid the on-site Marks and Spencer's food hall and when I return we tuck into sandwiches, crisps and cold drinks. Michelle is immersed in the Sunday paper and the girls are glued to their phones. I wander off and find a nurse, how long until the pharmacy get up here or can I collect on my way out? I am assured it's in hand and I have to wait until they deliver up to the ward, then and only then can I go. Remember me saying about inheriting my dad's lack of patience? I am quietly seething. I go into full moan mode in my room. Michelle and the girls are trying their hardest not to engage with me as I fume more and more. "I should have been out of here by lunchtime, what a waste of bloody time this is, completely buggered up all of your days, what's taking so long, it's only bloody painkillers and laxatives!" When the delivery guy shows up just after four-thirty I am ready to kill someone. I ask him why it took so long and he looks at me as if I have just asked him how the universe was first formed! Michelle scowls at me, the girls are slightly embarrassed, and we wave him off. A nurse pops in, quickly goes through the meds, what they are for and when to take them and finally, we can go. A porter arrives and I jump into his wheelchair. Off we go with me being pushed along, my overnight bag on my lap and the girls following behind. Once at the main reception I am deposited into one of the reception chairs while Michelle and the oldest one go and retrieve the car. Less than ten minutes later, I am loaded in the car with the three most important people in my life and heading for home. Made it.

I am so glad to be home, just to be surrounded by my own things and knowing someone's not going to be hassling me every two hours is bliss. This time I don't have to attend the local doctors surgery, I have dissolvable stitches that will go by themselves. There is no follow up other than the promise that I will be summoned for a scan in 3 months' time and issued with a follow up after that. I was discharged with pills and once those run out, that's it. No other meds, no chemo or radiotherapy, nothing. Once again, after the initial euphoria of being home the fatigue kicks in, big time! We're back to routine, friends pop in and pass on their best wishes, Michelle goes back to work and the girls get on with their lives. I find the constant tiredness a massive frustration and have to be reminded that I have just had my second stage three cancer operation. We manage to get our holiday in – a little normality.

Once again, the letter from Southmead arrives and it's first follow-up scan time again. I attend on my own and go through the usual motions. After 3 months I am bored and want desperately to get back to work, the fatigue is a lot better now but I am not at the level of being able to return to work just yet.

We get a letter stating that the consultation will be dealt with over the phone again. The call comes, introductions are made and we settle back for the results, listening via the speakerphone on my mobile. "The operation was a complete success; the scan shows that there is no cancer present anywhere," and we all agree that this is great news. "However" – I hate that bloody word – "Although you are clear at the moment we highly suspect, given the nature of the cancer, it will return. We can't say when but it appears inevitable, I am afraid." This news shocks us to the core. She gives us a moment and expresses her sympathies and tells us to take our time. We look at each other choked and try to think of questions that are relevant. I ask where they believe it will go next and she says it's highly likely it will be in my lymph glands or possibly my bones. The scans are being moved up to every six months now. She tells us we can call any time with any questions we might have and hangs up. This is not the news we were expecting. We are both in disbelief and have a cry, trying to console each other. Once we have discussed it, we agree to put on a united front, it's not what we were hoping for but right now I am clear and life is for living. We inform the girls, "Dad's beaten it twice, he can beat it again."

So, we practice what we preach. We all get on with life. I make my return to work in early November on another 'phased return' and we look forward to the Christmas festivities. It's good to have some normality in my life. I decide against returning to playing football, I am about to be fifty-three and perhaps it's time to hang up my boots for good. It's good to be around the other salespeople and nice to be back in a competitive environment, it helps to keep my brain busy. Life goes on as normal and in no time we are in 2020. I am working around fifteen hours a week now and getting stronger and stronger.

We get into late February; we've been quite busy which is really good and I am looking at a reasonable month for March. Although I have over thirty new cars ordered for this month, I am only going to be able to get around twenty of them if I am lucky. All of our new cars are made in plants that are mainly based in Europe and all of the Brexit nonsense is holding up shipping them to the UK so we are facing quite a backlog. This becomes much more apparent when we hear of something called Covid-19 which seems to be sweeping across Asia and mainland Europe. Factories

are being shut down and staff sent home and told to
isolate from one another as this Covid is an airborne
virus that is spreading rapidly and has flu like
tendencies but is far more dangerous and appears to
be a killer.

My 6 monthly scan comes around, a day that will
be forever etched in my memory: Tuesday, twenty-
fourth of March, 2020. I attend Southmead hospital
for an 8am appointment. I go through the normal
routine and make my way through what's left of rush
hour into central Bristol where I work. I am
welcomed by my colleagues; I finish helping out on
the pitch and get on with my day. I have my
fourteenth new car going out in about an hour and I
go and check that all is ready for when the customer
arrives. The rest of my morning goes without a hitch,
I'm waving my hopefully happy customer away in
their brand new twenty plate car (believe me, they will
be quite rare plates in the future) after going through
all of the controls with them and taking it for a little
test drive, tuning in their favourite radio stations and
pairing their phones. Once they're gone, I am called

in by the receptionist who says I have someone on the phone who wants to talk to me. Just as I start to engage in conversation with the person on the other line, my boss stands in front of me and says he wants me and all of the others in the sales team outside now. I try to make him realise I am on the phone but he repeats the word now and I realise this is something dramatic. I make my excuses, take down the caller's number and promise to call them back as soon as I can. We all assemble outside, there are about twelve of us in today including the three managers in the team. We get the news that the business (fourteen garage sites UK wide) has made the decision on Government advice to shut down due to the increased Covid-19 pandemic which is engulfing the UK and the world at large. We were all pretty shocked. We're told that we are going to be shut for at least the next 3 weeks but not to worry, we will all be paid as normal. To us this is completely alien, normally we are only closed for 4 days in the whole year! We are expected to call all of our customers that are due in to collect their new or used cars and to contact any appointments that we have and relay the news; everyone was going to be closing except for pharmacies, petrol stations and supermarkets.

We do as requested, then we are asked to clear the site. Logistically this is a huge headache. We have around one hundred and thirty new and used cars and vans on the pitch. Luckily, we have what we refer to as a 'large compound' where all of the new stock that comes in is delivered to. It's a secure site and we need to move some of that stock first before we can start stripping away at the units we have to move. We roll our sleeves up and get on with it. Everyone on the team pitches in and does their bit. We have to find room for all of the signage and flags that are attached to some of the vehicles and then it was shutters down, lights off, see you soon. The oddest drive home I have ever had. We live on the east side of Bristol; we are actually an equal distance in miles away from the centre of Bristol as we are to the centre of Bath. On my drive home that day, just after six in the evening, all of the streets were nigh on deserted. It was surreal to think we had no real idea of when we might return. Generally, we keep in touch by text and phone calls, and we watch every report on the news. There are jobs that need doing around the house so I busy myself with them, bearing in mind it's not that I am not used to being at home!

After the first 3 weeks of lockdown the government decrees that certain business sectors can reopen. Due to our service and repair arm, we are allowed to open on a limited basis. We are also allowed to continue to sell cars online but customers will have to wait on delivery until things calm down a little. The company texts and emails all of its staff, informing us that some staff will be asked to return but the majority of us will be placed on furlough. My boss calls me and says he is happy for me to be on furlough as it will give me a bit more time to complete my rehab from the last surgery. I am grateful for his suggestion and look forward to at least another 3 weeks off.

Just 2 days later we get the consultant's phone call again, not only from the cancer nurse specialist but she also has the Chief Urology Consultant with her – uh oh! "We're very sorry but your scan shows you now have a 10-millimetre lesion on the tail of your pancreas". Again? Give me a break! "We are aware you have not long had surgery but we feel it's imperative to get you in and have this removed as soon as it can be arranged. We are arranging for you to see a consultant in the Hepatobiliary clinic at the BRI and they will be in touch shortly."

JOURNEY NUMBER THREE

Michelle and I look at each other in shock. Hang on, I only had an operation 9 months ago, surely it can't be back that quickly. Bloody hell! We sit with a coffee and let it sink in. "Oh well, here we go again," I say and Michelle just looks at me. So once again we have to sit down with the girls and explain the latest news. They can't quite believe it, not again, you've only just had one! As usual I go into positive mode, "Well, that's the beauty of having a scan every 6 months, they have found it early and now we can deal with it." They both give me a cuddle; I can see that both of them are trying their hardest not to be upset in front of me. I know for a fact they both cried their hearts out later saying how unfair all this is and they were upset at the thought that I would have to go through it all again, especially so soon after the last operation. Michelle and I are more than aware that pancreatic cancer is generally a killer. Apparently, I am in luck with mine as the cancer is on the 'tail' rather than the 'head' and this can make all of the difference.

The next day I put a call in to my boss, he's in the Bristol branch but on a conference call. It's mid-morning, a gorgeous sunny day, and I decide to drive into work and deliver the news. Fifteen minutes later I am parking up and I get greeted by the couple of guys that have chosen not to be furloughed. They direct me inside as our boss is just finishing his call. He beckons me forward with a warm smile, genuinely pleased to see me, asks me how I am doing and then wishes he hadn't. He is very sympathetic and explains that I have no need to worry, my job is safe and I will continue to be paid. He asks me if there is anything I need and tells me to keep him in the loop. I tell him that while I am here, I will tell the others and he goes on to say they are spending the rest of the day digging all of the stock out that we locked away and renewing the pitch outside. That's a lot of work for only three people so I volunteer to help as I have nothing else to do and it will be nice to feel useful again. Once back outside in the sunshine I gather the others, tell them my news and that I am going to help out with the re-stock. I know they don't really know what to say so I crack a smile and ask them where all of the keys are. I head off in the direction of the compound and spend the rest of the afternoon feeling normal (something, at the time of writing this, I have not experienced since).

I am summoned to the BRI to meet my new consultant. This is a very odd experience. Michelle is with me; we park up in the nearest NCP and once out of the car, it's face masks on. On the way here there was very little traffic which is odd for a busy city centre like Bristol, it's usually rammed, thanks to our Lord Mayor. He's what I call a 'tree hugger', we once had a perfectly good solution for driving through and across the city centre but the area has now been revamped, made pretty and belongs the bicycle fraternity at the cost of millions to us council taxpayers. At one time you could drive across this city in around 20 minutes, now it's more like 3 days! As we walk toward the main reception of the hospital there are now temporary bollards up and signs everywhere relating to Covid. Only staff and people with appointments are allowed in, no visitors. There are a couple of security guards inside the entrance doors, they ask us our business and once satisfied, direct us to the hand sanitisers and disposable masks which we are encouraged to wear rather than the ones we have arrived in. We are familiar with the layout and head toward the main lift area. We head up to level four and find the ward we are supposed to be in. We book in at the small reception in front of us, it has a clear plastic screen all of the way across it, and we are asked to take a seat. The room is a fair size but due to the current 2-metre rule it's down to only about eight chairs. We have the choice of six of them and sit up against the back wall. Ten minutes or so pass and a nurse appears and calls my name. We both get up but she explains that only I can go through due to the Covid restrictions. She double checks who I am, date of birth and what I am there for. I am directed to a little room where there is a chair that doubles as a set of scales. I sit as requested, she records my weight, asks me my height, then peppers me with questions about smoking, drinking, any high blood pressure, any heart issues, any heart issues in the family, am I on any medication and if so what, and any allergies? Once all of this is sorted, I return to the reception. Shortly after this I am summoned again and this time led into a different room where I am greeted by my new consultant. He's in his early thirties, just transferred from London and originally from Holland. I ask him if Michelle can be present and he readily agrees. The nurse summons her forward and more introductions are made. We have a brief talk; he shows us the scan and explains what he plans to do. He examines me and asks about my general fitness, could I easily walk a mile, etc. He calls in his lead specialist nurse and introduces us. He explains that we have discussed the operation, the plan is to slice the cancer off the tail of my pancreas. This will be performed by keyhole surgery. We then get a warning that if this proves problematic, he will have to switch to open surgery and this will add to the time I am on the table. He wants her to deal with booking a bed in the ITU department for when I return from the operating theatre, then he goes through his operating schedule, selects the date – Tuesday, twenty-sixth of May, 2020 – and asks her to organise the pre-op. At this stage she asks us to just hang on a minute and disappears out of the room. We make small talk for a moment and she reappears smiling and says all done, come this way, we might as well do the pre-op now while you are here. Brilliant, let's do it.

We follow her out into the main corridor and she asks us if we are ok with the stairs, that we're only going two levels up – no problem. Ah, level six, been here before! She goes ahead and explains that I have only just been booked in. The nurse on the other side of the reception checks for me, nods her approval (at this point I can't see if she smiles because everyone is wearing a mask) and tells us to take a seat. In this one we can actually sit together as we are in the same 'bubble'. A young nurse pops her head around the corridor and calls my name. Michelle stays put and I follow the nurse into a room full of gadgets and a chair that can flatten out like a bed. We go through the usual round of questions and identification and then proceed to the ECG, blood pressure, temperature and bloods. When she is happy this is all done, she goes off and returns shortly with the pre-op 'shakes' – great, they taste bloody awful! We go through the do's and don'ts form and just as I am about to leave, she informs me that I will have to go for a Covid-19 swab test. She will arrange it now; it has to be done no more than forty-eight hours before the operation and will need to be negative in order for the operation to go ahead. I nod my thanks to her, collect Michelle on the way out and tell her the details of having to get a Covid test.

I have 10 days before the operation. Michelle is working from home and has taken over our kitchen, which is extended, turning it into a mini office. My eldest daughter has been taken off furlough and has returned to the accounts department in the same company I work for. My other daughter not only has me to worry about but she has just found out all of her GCSE exams have been cancelled and they are looking to grade them on the last set of mock exam results which she is devasted by because she has worked and studied so hard, she feels cheated. I get some quiet time and go through my bottom drawer. I fish out my funeral wishes from only 9 months ago and give it a quick scan. I change some of the music and even find time to download it on an old iPod. I make the decision to re-write the letters I had left for Michelle and both of the girls. Typical me, just in case.

Just when you think things generally can't get any worse, guess what? My eldest daughter comes home from work and tells me that I have a letter from the company. They have decided to streamline the business and made the decision to close two of their sites, one being where my daughter and I work. Really, you couldn't make this up. Everybody who currently works there will be invited to apply for certain vacancies that will be spread across three other sites that we have within the Bristol geographic area. However, there are only roughly twenty positions to fill and there must be at least one hundred and twenty people that work in our place. I get a letter the next day asking me to attend the first of two interviews to reapply for my existing job. My daughter has to go through the same process, the only problem is they are only offering three positions in the accounts section and there are eight of them applying. We certainly don't need this. I am more worried about her than I am me, she has been working there since she was fifteen. They took her into the accounts team just shy of a year ago where she has really shined. I tell her I am sure she will be fine and do my best to keep her confidence up.

My first interview is hilarious, I make the effort to wear a suit and company tie as I would normally wear, shined my shoes, you know, put a bit of pride into it. When I get there the others also in for their first interviews are dressed in shorts and t-shirts as it's a lovely warm day. But it's an interview! Mine is with my existing boss and we never discuss anything about work, he wants to know how I am, how Michelle and the girls are coping and tells me don't worry about anything, there will be a job for me. I chance my arm and cheekily mention my daughter, he just smiles and winks at me and says she is extremely well thought of, a good worker and I should be very proud of her, he was sure she would be alright. I get a text later that day informing me of when I should attend my second interview, which was when I would be in hospital. I make a call and speak to my boss's PA and she assures me not to worry, get the operation sorted and give us call when you are home and up to it, we will sort it all out then. Best of luck.

Two days later, Michelle comes with me as we drive into South Bristol and head towards Bristol City Football Club's ground, Ashton Gate. We have directions to be at what used to be known as the 'open end' that backs onto Ashton Park. We are due at eleven-thirty and we are a good 20 minutes early. We pull up at a mobile reception, have our letter scanned and are told to move forward. There are only two cars in front of us and there are distance warnings all over the place. We get beckoned forward and asked to wind the window down. I am faced with what I presume is a nurse who is dressed head to toe in PPE but she looks like she is at the site of a nuclear disaster with her clumpy boots and plastic visor covering her face. From a packet, she produces a single swab; it looks like an extremely long ear bud. It gets pushed up my right nostril, then my left. It feels like it's gone up so far it's hitting my brain! I get the command to open my mouth and another one goes to the back of my throat making me gag. That's it, done, you can go now. We drive home with another new little story to recount.

Yet again we enjoy a family evening; Chinese takeout and a movie, this seems to be our ritual now. The girls are doing their best to not show their emotions and I tell them I am going to be ok. This is going to be really weird; I am not allowed any visitors due to the Covid restrictions, none. This time they have also not given any indication as to how long I am going to be in hospital for. I promise to try and FaceTime when I can, I am working on the presumption that may be tomorrow night but more likely to be the day after on the Wednesday.

Again, we are due to book in on level six at seven in the morning. I follow the printed instructions as normal, no food digested since the evening before and both the 'lovely' shakes consumed at the appropriate time earlier that morning. This time our eldest daughter has the day off and offers to take us down, that way Michelle won't have to worry about parking the car or how long she is going to be there. There's nervous chatter as we drive into Bristol in her cramped little three-door Citroën. We are there in no time, not just because it is so early but also the Covid restrictions have the majority of people staying at home in lockdown. Michelle and I get out, my daughter kisses me goodbye and wishes me luck and says to Michelle that she is going to hang on for a bit and to call her if she is going to be staying for any amount of time. She stays parked right outside the main reception in one of the few spaces that are there, perfect.

We mask up and continue inside. We make it past the security, use the hand sanitisers and head along the long corridor for the array of lifts. We jump in one, hit the button for level six and away we go. Once we exit the lift we turn left, walk along the corridor and then there is a slight slope that leads up to the reception that we are to report to. We are stopped before we get there. A nurse holding a clipboard is booking everybody in, trying to preserve the 2 metre distance between everyone. Now I have been ticked off her list, she looks at Michelle and tells her she can go no further due to Covid. I can see the upset in her eyes, I puff out my chest, draw her into my arms, cuddle her and tell her I love her and I am going to be fine, go on, I will see you soon. I am beckoned to move forward where another nurse is waiting to guide me into the little waiting rooms that they have there. I look behind me as Michelle makes her way back out and we have a final wave and then she's gone.

I settle in my room as instructed and wait for the next command. A few minutes later another nurse pops her head around the pulled curtain that separates me from the rest of the world. She introduces herself and goes through the usual round of questions. I am given my two identity tags and she then leaves a pair of the 'flight socks' to be fitted once I change into my gown. She leaves me to do this and promises to return in a couple of minutes. When she's back she takes an inventory of what is in my overnight bag and writes out a tag for that too. I am encouraged to wear either slippers or 'sliders' as I will be walking to the theatre when it's my turn. I ask when I am due down for the op', she says she is not sure as the list has quite a few on today. My 'socks' are fitted, the anaesthetist will be along soon, pull the chord if you need anything. I can hear other people in nearby cubicles getting their instructions and I sit back and get to grips with today's news on my smartphone.

This is the first time that I have been left on my own before a major operation and I will be honest, it's a little unnerving. When the anaesthetist turns up I'm so happy to have some sort of interaction and I think he picks up on my slight nervousness. He is great, takes me through what is going to happen, tells me if all goes well it's going to be two or three hours, and they're not sure at this stage when they will come for me, it's looking like late morning. He makes his excuses and leaves to go to his next patient. At this stage it's only around seven-thirty in the morning, I've got the feeling this is going to be a long day. I text Michelle the update and I return to the news on my phone. Michelle texts me back and we carry on with our little conversation across the morning. One of the nurses pops in around ten and encourages me to have a small drink of water as they are concerned that I might get dehydrated. I brought the latest John Grisham with me (my favourite author) and manage to get through the first six chapters when they tell me it's my turn next, a porter is on his way up to collect me. I hastily turn off my phone and put it and my book (and reading glasses, old age you know!) into my bag. A youngish chap appears and asks me if I am ready to go? "Yep, bring it on," and away we go, again! He leads me down to the theatre block. He deposits me with the theatre team, promising to take care of my overnight bag, it will be with you when you are taken to your ward. I thank him and he is gone. This time there were no real introductions, other than the familiar presence of the anaesthetist I had no other interaction with anyone. This time not only did I have to walk to theatre, no pushed on a bed, no wheelchair, no little anti-room with introductions and all smiley faces with explanations of what was to come but I was asked to actually walk into the operating theatre itself and was given the instruction to hop on the bed! I remember parking my sliders together at the bottom of the theatre bed and thinking how cold it was in the room. Blooming hell, it's all gone downhill since my first operation just over five years ago. They ask me the usual questions to establish that they are about to perform the right operation on the right person. I have various cannulas put into my arm and my left hand, they manhandle me into the correct position for this surgery and bang, I'm out for the count. Michelle, once again, is going to fill in the next bit.

Despite knowing that I am not going to be able to wait with him until they are ready to collect for the operation, as I have always done before, it is still a bit of a shock when we reach level six and I am turned away from going onto the reception area. After he confirms his details with a nurse holding a clipboard, he turns, we embrace, said our 'love you's' and I remember him saying, "Call you later." After a few steps I look back and just before he disappears around the corner, I catch a last wave. I take a few deep breaths and get the lift back down to the main reception. Thinking about it, I did well to get past the security they have on the front door! My daughter is still parked in the place where she had dropped us off only about ten minutes earlier. I explain what has happened so far and we drive home, trying to think of a cup of tea and some breakfast to keep our minds from what is going on.

Both the girls are home today, it is turning out to be a gloriously warm sunny day. We have all of the windows and the double-glazed doors that lead out to the back garden open. The dog is wandering in and out, as she does. There's music coming from the youngest's USB speaker and I am busying myself cleaning around the house. It amuses the girls as they always say that I do this every time he is in having an operation, they call it 'mum nesting'. Late in the morning my sister-in-law turns up for moral support, that's typical of her. I explain that we have exchanged a few texts, the last one around elevenish, but I have not heard yet if he has gone down for the operation. My youngest says she has been invited out with her friends and I encourage her to go. We can't do anything here and I promise to call her if I hear anything. The kettle's on and we sit out in the sun and chat aimlessly away whilst I keep one eye on my mobile phone.

It's getting on for one p.m. and I have not had any more

texts. I want to text him but I figure he has been taken down to surgery and I convince myself I will hear something in due course. We have a nice lunch and continue to take advantage of the sun. It's after four and still no news. My sister-in-law makes a move and returns home and I chat nervously to my oldest whilst we muse over what the youngest one is up to. It's just past five now, I haven't heard from him for almost six hours. The surgery was planned to be two to three hours so I decide to 'hit the phones' as my husband would say. We knew he was going to be sent to the ITU ward after his op so I call them. After a few rings I manage to talk to somebody who is very helpful and they confirm that he is not on the ward at this moment and ask if they can put me on hold to see where he is. My heart is in my mouth for a few moments and it seems like an eternity until they come back on the line. "He's still in resus." Thank god! My mind has been racing and with the girls both looking at me for answers, I at least have something positive to share with them. I am asked to call back a little later which I readily agree to do and ring off with some relief. I get several calls and texts from friends and I update everybody including calling my sister-in-law. She gets in a bit of a muddle as she is not very techie and her husband Graham wants to hear every word so a little debate goes on while they sort out how to get it on speakerphone, this way, he says, "She can't get it wrong!" Bless her.

We have a little bite to eat and I decide as it's been over an hour since my last call, he must be on the ward by now so I put in another call. I get a different nurse on the phone and after a short while I am informed that he is still in resus which really concerns me as he had been there for such a long time. They agree to ring me as soon as he is brought up to the ward and I have no choice but to agree and thank them for their help. I bring the girls up to date with the latest and we try our best to get on with things whilst waiting on a phone call.

Sometime after seven I get a call and it's from his consultant/surgeon who explains that he is ok and on his way up to ITU now. The surgery didn't go the way they were hoping and it proved impossible to slice the tumour away from his pancreas. They ended up switching to open surgery and cutting away a section of the pancreas itself and because it was what they call 'soft', it was leaking pancreatic juice and they had to fit a drain to it. This was not to be a permanent fixture and would hopefully be removed in a few days. He went on to say he had been made aware of my earlier calls and he had just scrubbed out of surgery and wanted to put my mind at rest. I thank him profusely. He says he will look in on him in the morning and if there is anything else I need then please call ITU.

Wow, talk about relief. I share the news with the girls that their dad is fine and should be up on the ward now. As we all start texting those who are desperate to hear how things are going, I get another 'unknown number' call on my phone. I answer with slight trepidation and a lady introduces herself as one of the ward doctors from ITU, "Your husband is now with us. We are making him as comfortable as we can, he is very sleepy and we will let him rest but keep a close eye on him. Just wanted you to know as I was made aware of your earlier calls." I pass on my gratitude to her and her team and agree to call in the morning. What a day.

The next week was pretty much the strangest in all of my thirty-two years of being with him. In the past we would go and visit, take in goodies to compensate for the variation of food (that was very pc of me) and generally help to lift his spirits. But this is Covid-19, there's no visiting allowed by anyone and it feels so wrong knowing that he is so ill and we are not able to comfort him. It's almost cruel – no, it is cruel. I call the ward first thing the following morning and am told he is awake; he is with his consultant at the moment but I am told they would pass on that I have called. Much later in the morning he manages to call, I can hear upset in his voice, not like him at all. He only speaks for a few seconds, confirms he is ok but really tired and will call back later.

The first time he FaceTimed us was a shock, he was so pale, like he had lost a load of weight and just looked so knackered. He couldn't keep the call going for long as he just was not up to it. I think we all realised that this surgery had been the most invasive for him so far we thought it best to wait on his calls rather than constantly disturb him. I know the girls both sent him the odd text and I know that he responded to them almost immediately. I am in the queue in Aldi when he phones me – typical – but he calls me back a little later. I try to put his mind at rest, we are all fine, getting on with things, no need to worry about us. I can tell he isn't his normal self, in fact I have never known him sound so quiet, it is almost like he is depressed. I think he just feels helpless as he is stuck in there with no real idea of what is going on in the world.

I have to update his brother daily, he desperately wants to go in and see him but I have to keep saying even I can't see him, all because of Covid. We both feel so hopeless and, to a great *degree, even guilty. I, better than anyone, know how stubborn and strong my husband is and his ability to have an unbending will but I am truly worried about him. I speak to someone on the ward about my concerns and they assure me they were keeping a close eye on him and that they can provide people to go in and talk to him if he wants. I am working on the presumption that they asked him and he said no, I am fine. That's him!*

Getting his call on the following Monday that he is coming home is fantastic news, if a little daunting. He makes me aware of all of the medications he is expected to take and that there will be injections to be done daily as well. I am concerned that he is coming out of ITU straight to home and he has not rested on a normal ward but I can sense how desperate and excited he is to be coming home.

When we eventually pick him up (what a stressful day that was), I have never seen him look so small and vulnerable. My heart sinks and I exchange looks with my youngest who was home and excited to come and collect him, and she looks as shocked as I am. We both put a brave face on it and scoop him up from his wheelchair and deposit him and his large array of bags into the car. I will be honest and say I am not prepared in the slightest for how broken he looks and when he gets upset on the way home, I am really worried about his recovery. As usual, once at home his strength returns, he digs in deep, never showing any of us his pain and battles hard against the awful physical challenges of the pancreas drain, even when it becomes infected. The relentless taking of all of those different drugs, the daily injections and blood pressure tests are so overwhelming and to this day I do not know how he dealt with it with so much humility and, at times, humour, but he did. This is the third time he has come through it, I can see it has changed him a little but he is as tough as old boots and will face the next challenge, if there is one, face on, as will we.

I can hear people moving about, lots of people. There's some laughter coming from somewhere and I can hear beeping sounds. I try to open my eyes but it is a real struggle. I appear to be in a dark gloomy area. I try to focus. I am definitely not in a room, it appears I am parked up in a corridor. One of the nurses must notice me and comes over calling me by my first name and asking me if I know where I am. Darkness, I am unconscious again. I am woken up some time later, it might have even been just after my earlier recollection, I have no idea. I am heavily sedated and surrounded by an ITU ward doctor and two nurses. I have a thermometer placed in my ear and a blood pressure armband attached. They explain what they are doing and check the meds that are being pumped into me through one of the cannulas in my arm. The doctor goes on to explain that the surgeon had to fit a drain to my pancreas which was not in the original plan so at this point I presume all did not go as planned but I am too worn out to press him further for details. He tells me that he has called Michelle and assured her I am through the operation and am now being monitored up on the ward. He says he gave her the direct ward phone number and she promised to call in the morning. They slip a mask over my face for oxygen, this will help me in my immediate recovery and to breathe easier if any pain kicks in. I realise I am in what I would call an old-fashioned ward. It's basically a large room where beds have been placed, with lots of machines including a keyboard, mouse and flat screen scattered around and extendable tripod style lights that pull down from above. I have a heart monitor attached and it incessantly beeps. I am in the far left of this room so to my immediate left is a wall but it has a window, almost like a serving hatch. I can see through and it appears to be another area like I am in. I have a long curtain which is closed and separating me from whoever is in the next bed and another floor to ceiling curtain in front of me which is, at the moment, only partially drawn. This is where the staff are coming in from. On my only wall is a large, white, rectangular clock. It looks like the type you see in railway stations, numbered one through to twelve, one large minute hand and one smaller for the hour and a slim, long ever-moving second hand. Underneath it in a big bold font is today's day and date, TUESDAY 26 MAY 20. It's just after nine and it suddenly dawns on me that I went into surgery at around eleven-thirty this morning and it was only supposed to be two to three hours max!

Fatigue hits hard and I am away again. I get the obs treatment, the pricking of the fingers for blood sugar levels is definitely the worst bit. I am not sure how often this is happening but I think it is safe to say with quite some regularity. At some point they take the oxygen mask from me and I doze off yet

again. I am woken by a loud beeping/alarm, one of
the nurses rushes in, replaces the oxygen mask and
monitors me for a while. She resets the alarm and I
drift off once more. The morning comes really early
in ITU. There is a shift change at seven in the
morning and it is evident that the new staff are mostly
there at least 30 minutes before for briefings and
handovers. There is a flurry of activity and people
everywhere. My entrance/exit curtain has been drawn
all the way back and now I have a better idea of
where I am. To the right of my slightly curtained off
view is the nurses' station, it is quite long and littered
with various computer screens along its entire length.
I count at least six people sitting either fixated on a
screen or talking on one of the many telephones that
are fighting for space along the surface. There are
others stood behind, holding files and clipboards and
yet more at each end, clustered into groups, some
holding water bottles, others a mug of something.
Behind all of this is a really large whiteboard, I focus
on it for a moment and four rows down, there is my
name.

Later, when I get up and about, I work out there
are only ten beds on the ward, they are constantly full
and the patients' names, bed number, date of
operation, how many operations they have had whilst
still in ITU and number of days in are all recorded for
everyone to see. The other things that become
apparent from my new 'resting place' (what a laugh
that turned out to be) was that any spent or unwanted
piece of machinery or empty bed or wheelchair gets
parked right opposite my bed! To make things even
better, one of the entrance ways into the ward was
attached to the only wall I had, these doors opened
with regularity that I wonder why they bothered
fitting them at all. It seems that not only is there a
large staff in ITU all of the time but it is obviously a
shortcut to other wards with all sorts of staff coming
through at all times of the day. I have to say, I find
this exhausting as I really need to rest, this was my
second major operation in less than 9 months, this is
the first time I have not had my own room. There is
no TV, no adjoining bathroom and to add insult to
injury the first time I need a wee I am forced to
relieve myself into one of those odd shaped

cardboard bottles as I am not allowed out of bed yet. Just to add to my overwhelming exhaustion, let alone my impatience levels, the chap in the next bed turns out to be a bloody nightmare. I don't know what he is in for but I remember coming across him in the pre-op ward yesterday when we were all being booked in for our operations. A little older than me but looks more like twenty years older than me. Very loud and with a really strong Bristolian accent. I vividly remember the nurses asking him if he had managed to give up smoking as he had been advised, with his almost mute missus – there acting as his care person – nodding her disapproval and saying, "Oh, no." At this point he is coughing and wheezing his guts out and now, lucky me, he is the other side of my noise-proof curtain (not!) attached to the noisiest air machine that makes a loud gagging and hissing noise constantly. The devices he is hooked up to are bleeping nonstop. As the days go by, this guy has to be constantly attended to, he can't take a sip of water on his own. He has to be helped to be fed, he has constant bed baths and even when I eventually left he still had not moved from his bed. I'll be honest, I could have bloody killed him, what a pain in the arse!

Breakfast arrives on my first morning at around seven-thirty which seems really late compared with all of the early morning activity here. I wave the trolley lady off. She presses me for a lunch and dinner order but I am really not up to it so I just ask for a sandwich or something. This seems to satisfy her and off she goes. I was introduced to my new day nurse earlier and he pops over to make sure I am ok, explains that the consultant will be in to see me at about eight and continues with his first obs of the day for me. I have various pills that I have to take now along with the usual array of painkillers and laxatives. One of these is called Creon and I have to take three of them three times a day after food, every day for the rest of my life. These are to help break down the nutrients in my body, something my pancreas was taking care of before some of it got removed. He also tells me that my overnight bag has just been delivered, apparently at some point they had misplaced it but it's now sitting on my not-to-be-used-by-a-visitor visitor seat. I ask him to pass it over and grab my phone and charger, at this point I am not interested in anything else. There is a bag of pound coins and a debit card in there, some changes of clothes including what I wore in yesterday, my John Grisham and my toiletries. I put my phone onto the tray beside me with the plastic water beaker and cup, and close my eyes. The consultant and the anaesthetist are now both standing at the bottom of my bed. The consultant finishes reading my chart and asks me how I am feeling whilst examining my stomach area. He tells me that things went a little differently to how they had hoped and it proved impossible to slip the cancer off the pancreas as previously planned. They ended up switching to an open surgery procedure and had to remove a larger section of my pancreas. Because of this, it became necessary to fit a drain to the pancreas itself, hence the tube hanging out of my left torso and the line attached to a bag that was in a cage at the bottom of my bed. He answers my next question before I ask it, "It's only temporary, might be a couple of days, could be a week or so, just depends on how much the pancreas needs to leak after the assault that's just happened on it." He reminds me that when I get up on my feet, and he really wants that to happen today if I feel up to it, to take the drain with me! He then goes on to say that the operation went on for longer than anticipated but he got it all. He was made aware that my wife had called in a couple of times and was, of course, worried. Once he'd finished and scrubbed out he put a call into her to reassure her that I was ok and now up on the ward where they would take care of me overnight. I thank him for this. I notice that not only did I have this drain stuck to me but also a couple of horizontal black lines across the left side of my chest and stomach. He tells me they were from having to switch to the open surgery, they were incisions which he had 'glued' shut rather than stitched. "They're going to leave a mark, but nothing drastic." Both of them seemed pleased with their work, "Try and get up and about if you can," and they promise to see me the following morning. Shortly after this one of the young doctors comes over to say my wife had called to see how I am, she told her I was doing ok and was with the consultant at the moment. She said she will call later. I thank her for this and send a quick 'Morning' text message as this is all I have the strength for.

On my next obs I am introduced to another nurse, a middle-aged woman who clearly loves her job. She chats away incessantly whilst explaining that she is here to fit me with some 'slipper socks' so that I don't slip as she is going to get me up out of bed and walking. Get me up, she does, bless her. I have a lovely pair of orange/olive fluffy ankle socks on over my 'flight' socks. She gently gets me in a sitting position, helps me to swing my legs out over the left side of the bed and passes me the drain which is collecting 'juices' from my pancreas. I have to say, I am slightly concerned as the bag is half full and it's a dark brownish liquid that doesn't look particularly appealing. She helps me up and I take a few tentative steps out into the busy corridor. She asks if I am ok and I assure her I am. She encourages me a little further and then says that's enough, she does not want to tire me out. I get back to my bed and she helps arrange me back in. The chart at the bottom of my bed is updated and she asks me to try and go for more walks, three or four times a day if possible, and to also not spend all day in bed. She pats the visitor chair and says spend some time in here.

The routine continues with more obs. Lunch arrives bang on twelve o' clock. I opt for a ham sandwich and some ice cream. I get up and go for a little stroll, I go left and after about 20 feet there is a toilet/shower. It's empty and I decide I will try and go to the toilet. After a bit of a strain, I manage to go for a wee, nothing's happening elsewhere! I wash my hands, use the drier and make my way back to my 'room'. Once I have got my breath back, I FaceTime Michelle. They are all in our kitchen having lunch, I can see that it's a beautiful bright sunny day, they're all in shorts and vests. One of the worst things about being in the ITU ward was how glum it was. You only realised it was night time because the glumness went to a new level of even glummer. They are thrilled to see me, well actually, I think they are all a bit shocked seeing me in my gown with my drain hanging off me and although I really want to talk, I immediately get choked for some reason but they are certainly glad to have a chat. Michelle does her best to tell me about yesterday's events but I tire quickly and she can see I am really struggling physically and emotionally. "Why don't you call us back when you are feeling stronger, we're all ok and missing you. Don't worry about us, we're fine." I manage to clamber back into bed and fall straight to sleep.

My alarm is going, at some point they put the oxygen back on me as my breathing was laboured and I have somehow knocked it off. It was a little frightening to wake up like that and even more so that it keeps happening. A doctor rushes over and does a quick examination, he advises that I keep the mask on for a little while longer. Every time I go into a deep sleep my blood pressure falls to an alarming state, this happened when trying to come around on my previous operation and it also happened when they were resuscitating me this time. It was another reason why it took so long to get me up on the ward. The doctor orders one of the nurses to gather some more blankets and I am wrapped up with them and the oxygen mask is put back on. With everybody rushing about I am missing having a bit of conversation. Also, with everyone in PPE and masks you can't even see someone smiling at you. I am feeling more than a little isolated being here. It's really weird that I have had two previous occasions whereby I was alone in my own room all day apart from a little bit of visiting and here I am in the middle of a crowd and I have never felt so lonely – bizarre!

My late afternoon obs have a little surprise for me, not only is it all of the usual fun things washed down with a load of pills but now I have to have a blood thinning injection placed in the bottom of my stomach. I am ok with needles so it doesn't bother me, however it is then explained that I will have to have this every day for the next month – great! Tea arrives, it's another sandwich and ice cream again as I still really don't fancy much. I make an effort to eat what I can and then go for my afternoon stroll. I try the bathroom again, this time with much more success with the peeing, that all seems fine but still no news from the other end. I decide to call Michelle, it's easier on me than the FaceTime. For some reason I can feel myself getting upset again, what's that all about? We manage to have a bit of a chat; she explains to me in more detail about what happened yesterday and how worried she was because the last time we communicated by text was around eleven in the morning and when there was nothing further she presumed, rightly as it turned out, that I had gone down for surgery. Once it started heading towards four o' clock, worry started to set in. That's when she hit the phones and it took a little while to find out what was going on and where I was. She expressed her thanks to not only the ward doctor for calling her but the consultant for taking the time to do so as well. I manage a quick word with our youngest, the older one is out with friends. I ring off saying I will call tomorrow and find somewhere I can plug my charger in. This has completely knackered me out and it's not long before I am out for the count again.

After a whole day of not really talking to anyone, being woken what seems like every five minutes and the forever ongoing noise from the bed next door, I am beginning to get a little rattled. The morning shift change is going on and it's so noisy, I'm bloody knackered, don't these people know I need some rest? The new nurse comes in and I bite her head off. Once she has done what she needs to she retreats to the nurses' station where I have no doubt she is complaining about me. Last night was truly horrendous, not only did I have to listen to the neighbour from hell gagging all night but so many people seemed to be around the nurses' station, it was like a pop-up party was going on. The lights were shining through and over my curtains and I really struggled to settle down. The breakfast trolley arrives, yesterday I just asked for some orange juice but this morning I am ravenous. I break into a smile and ask for toast and marmalade and a cup of tea. The smile vanishes when the trolley lady says we don't do toast, just cereal. I replied well, you did 9 months ago when I was in the Thoracic ward. She looks at me and said only cereals. So, I reluctantly ask for Frosties, she looks at me and says we only have cornflakes, Rice Crispies or Weetabix. So, I ask her for a bowl of cornflakes, smothered with sugar, then milk and a cup of tea. These NHS cutbacks are killing me! She pulls a menu out for lunch and asks what I would like. I scan it and think, oh wow, they do an all-day breakfast for lunch, yes please. Big mistake, it is awful. After that, I have to admit, I stuck to the sandwich selection both for lunch and tea.

My second full day there starts getting better

when, just after eight, my consultant and anaesthetist are back. They engage me in some conversation which is wonderful, my notes are shared and checked, I get a quick examination and they check the pancreatic drain. They seem quite pleased with everything, including me being up and about and having some success in the toilet area. The consultant tells me that they are going to get me on the ward today if possible and I cannot conceal my joy at moving out of here. Routine continues across the day, my obs continue, I am encouraged to continue for a bit longer with the oxygen if I am planning on going to sleep. I have my little walks, sit in the chair and give the toilet I found another visit. It takes some concerted effort but I get there in the end, success, brilliant, something else I can tell the doctors. At some point I FaceTime Michelle, my oldest daughter is back to work but my youngest one joins in the call. They are pleased to see I look a lot better; I say it's down to the bed bath I was given this morning and they both laugh. I tell them that it is a nightmare here trying to get any sleep, but it is planned I will be on a ward soon, I can't wait and I promise to call them with the details of where I go next. I say I will try and call again later when the oldest one is home and hang up. Late afternoon arrives, more obs, more pills and another injection. I ask about being moved and I am told there are no free beds on the wards at the moment but they will move me as soon as they can. I am more than a little disappointed, I just hope tonight isn't like last night. To be fair it isn't, it is far worse!

Whoever is across from me at the nurses' station must have invited at least one friend each. It is so noisy, it's crazy. Because most of the patients are presumably asleep, there appears to be less for the night shift staff to do so they all congregate around the nursing station just to the right of my 'room'. The guy next door is ramping up his gagging and his oxygen machine must have a bloody turbo attached to it, it is so loud – give me strength. It doesn't help that I am generally a light sleeper. In between the obs I pass out through shear tiredness. Friday begins in the same manner as the day before. Shift change, same nurse as I had on Wednesday, obs done, breakfast arrives, oh the choice, same again. The consultant arrives in his own this time, checks me over, we have a quick chat, he says he is slightly concerned with the amount of liquid that is still seeping out into the drain from the pancreas. He apologises that I have not been moved to a ward yet, the hospital is full, but promises that as soon as a bed becomes free, it's mine. I ask him if there is any chance of going home as it's Friday today and I would love to be home for the weekend. He frowns at me and says that he would want me to rest up here for at least another few days. I try my hardest to conceal my disappointment. The Covid restrictions on visitors and not having Michelle and the girls around me is hitting me a lot harder that I thought it ever would. Otherwise, the consultant feels I am making excellent progress and he promises to see me tomorrow, a Saturday and they are still going to try and move me on to a ward. This placates me for now and I carry on as I really have no other choice.

My routine carries on pretty much how I have described over the weekend, although the issue with needing the oxygen has abated. I am massively disappointed to not be able to go home, especially as I could see when Facetiming that the weather out there is gorgeous and I love the sun and the warm. One thing that is slightly exciting is that I manage to discover two vending machines on one of my longer walks. I make my way back to ITU, rummage about in my bag and find my little bag of pound coins. It takes me a few minutes to get going again but it feels like being a kid on Christmas morning when I return with my little bounty, a real proper full fat can of Coke and a grab bag of Cheddars – result!

There are two significant things that really affect me that happen over the weekend. The first one, which I am going to recount in a minute, upset me so much that when I eventually get out of hospital it takes me 3 days and several attempts before I can tell Michelle about it as I was so caught up in the narrative it was difficult to get it out. The Saturday morning arrives and, as promised, my consultant comes in to check me over and another hardy breakfast (not) was consumed. Now that I am moving around a bit more I have managed to get a good idea of the layout of the ward. The 'parking ' wall opposite me is the retaining wall to another area like the one I

137

am in with another six beds. While walking around I am able to see that all of these beds are full, as are the three that are to the right of me. After I pass by my mate, Mr Noisy, the next 'room' has all the curtains drawn across apart from the very end one. I can't make out the patient very well but there are a couple of young female nurses chatting away and I realise by the name they are referring to that it's a female patient. They look like they are getting her ready for something, there's talk of make-up and clothes and one of them is clearly tending to her hair. I turn and double back past the nurses' station and glance up at the big white board. There is only one female on the ward, the board states that she is now on day fifty-five of being on the ward and has had five operations in that time. The poor thing. Just around two, the nurses unhitch her bed and push her past me and they don't return for a good couple of hours. I found out later that she was a bit younger than me, had only recently married and had got to the point of no return with her illness. They had arranged for her husband to see her in the open-air roof garden for a couple of hours as she did not have much more time. I am so glad it was such a beautiful afternoon for them. When she was rolled back in past me, I could see on her face how happy she was through her tears, it's something I will never forget.

Much later on that Saturday evening, I am sat up in the visitor chair, trying my hardest to concentrate on the John Grisham I brought in with me. I like to read, but I love to read anything by Mr Grisham. At the time of writing this I have a copy of every title he has ever published except for the Ebook stuff; I am old-fashioned when it comes to reading, I like to physically turn a page and have the comfort that comes from owning the book. I have read and re-read these more times than I can remember. A new to me young, pretty looking doctor comes over and introduces herself. She has a Liverpudlian accent. She asks me hop up onto the bed and peppers me with questions while she goes on to examine me. Once all that's done, she fills out my chart and seems in no hurry to leave. I ask her if she is enjoying her role here and she says it is part of her rotation so tonight's her first night on ITU and I am her first patient. I say that she's a long way from home, I can hear in your voice that you are originally from Liverpool. I can just about see her beam a smile from under her face mask and she concludes that yes she is, from Kirkby, in fact. "Red or Blue?" She looks at me and says, "Red". I pull up my right sleeve and reveal my Everton tattoo and she laughs, "Oh sorry." I laugh and tell her not to worry about it. She asks me why I support them considering I am not from the area and I won't bore you all with it as it is a long story but it's been my football club since I was 8 years of age. We talk about Bristol; she asks me where I live and we talk about the neighbourhoods that I wouldn't necessarily want to live in. She has been here for about 4 months, renting a little place on the dock front and has fallen in love with the place. Great nightlife, friendly people and reminds her of home. She tells me that she is buying a place of her own in Clifton and can't wait for it all to go through. I wish her luck and she promises to look in on me later. We didn't get the opportunity to talk again but she will never know how grateful I was to have some interaction and conversation at what was probably my lowest time. Saturday night stuck in hospital with absolutely no-one is without doubt the loneliest I have ever felt in my life, I just want to go home.

Sunday, routine, routine, routine. I am bored out of my head. If I didn't have this damn drain attached to me, I think I would have just walked out. I have really, really had enough. It's a long day and quite honestly, I will be glad to see the back of it. Night draws in, the lights get dimmed and the usual night time hustle begins. I come to, it's dark but I have the feeling that it is just before morning is about to break. I decide to get up. I really want to have a shower, I have been here for six days now and not had a shower yet. I get up, look for my overnight bag and reach down to remove my toiletries and a towel. As I go to get up, I reach out and put my weight on what I thought was a radiator bolted to the wall. It turns out it was some sort of plastic cover, it couldn't take the load, it slid away under my hand and dumped me flat on my arse! All hell breaks loose, several nurses rush in and want to know if I am ok? What was I doing? What was I thinking of? Why didn't you call for one of us? They usher me back into bed and once I tell them about going for a shower I feel like a scolded little boy when they say not at one-thirty in the morning you are not! Back to sleep, bad boy.

Monday morning eventually breaches the perimeter that is the ITU. It's just after five and I head for the shower. The toilet I have been using is in a much larger room that also has a walk-in shower that, while appearing pretty basic, I have been admiring over the last couple of days. I twist the lock on the door, go to the loo and then strip off all of my hospital garb. Surprise, surprise the water is cold, I step back and let it run for a bit. I am convinced that I have turned the temperature control up to the maximum but it makes no difference. Sod it, I am minging, just get it done. Bloody hell, it's cold!

Re-dressed, back to my bed and things packed away, a nurse comes in and explains that not only is she here to do my obs but to make a report about my fall in the night. I explain to her that it is not worth making a big deal over but according to her, it is. She files her report with me, making light of it and it all goes into my notes. The consultant shows up again with the anaesthetist in tow. He is aware of my adventure last night and explains that this could hold me up going home as it is hospital policy that they monitor for another 24 hours after any fall. I explain that I didn't really fall, I overbalanced and only dropped by a foot, if that. He looks at me and can see that I am fine, there's still no space on the wards and at this point I just ask him outright to go home. He looks at his colleague and they step away and discuss it. "Ok, you will need to be able to dress the wound around your pancreas drain and attend my surgery here at the BRI for me to monitor it and hopefully remove it once it dries up." Where do I sign – yippee! – I am getting out of here today. He calls over one of the ward doctors and shares what we have discussed. He returns to let me know they will organise my discharge for today and I will only be able to leave once the pharmacy put together all of my meds. They both wish me well and he tells me he will see me on Thursday at ten-thirty in the morning. He will get a letter sent out today to confirm. He signs off on my chart and is gone. I text Michelle immediately. I am so happy to be going home. After a few texts back and forth I agree to call when I know a bit more about when this is likely to happen, Michelle replies - "anytime". A nurse appears and asks me to start thinking about getting dressed and did I need any help. She's an older lady and I have not seen her before. She explains that she is an agency nurse and she has worked on this ward many times before. She said she would be back in ten minutes and would go through my medicine regime which is quite extensive. I excitedly dress, grab all of my gear and place it in my bag, put my debit card and a couple of quid in my denim shorts pocket and gather up my mobile phone and charger.

As promised, she returns and goes through all of the medicines that I am going to have to take over the next 30 days. She is lovely, she takes the time to write down what to take and when, all of the way through the day. For the first 14 days I am on 43 pills and an injection each day. I have to prove I can inject myself and until they are satisfied that I can, they will not let me leave. She carefully takes me through the procedure and although it is earlier than normal, I inject myself with no problems whatsoever. Once home, I let Michelle do this, she loved it! We go over everything once more then she goes off and returns with a wheelchair and we're off. I only make it about 30 feet and I get parked up in an empty ward. They need my bed and the plan is to leave me here until the pharmacist appears. The ward I am on is freezing, I am only wearing shorts and a t-shirt and I don't have anything else. After about half an hour the kindly nurse swings by to check on me. She can see I am a little uncomfortable and organises a blanket for me. It's late morning, I call Michelle and we have a little chat. She knows I am desperate to come home but tells me not to worry, we are here ready to pick you up whenever. Just before midday another nurse happens by and asks if I would like to be included for lunch. She seems to think I should so I agree and she says she will ring down and organise something. Lunch arrives and is gratefully consumed. I update Michelle by text and then I am overcome with tiredness and drop off into a nap. I am woken gently by a lady with a clipboard. She identifies herself as somebody from the pharmacy department and is here to double-check all of these meds that I need. Once

she is happy, she says she will get them organised and
brought up. I ask how long and she replies about an
hour or so. It's just after two in the afternoon, great,
hopefully I will be away around three. I call Michelle
and give her the latest news. It's almost four when
some goofy chap turns up with my medicine bags. I
am fuming, I have been here all bloody day waiting
on this numpty! I take them off him and then walk
back to the ward I was on, saying I am ready to go.
They organise a porter for me and I call Michelle to
come down, I am told to tell her that it will be from
the collection point at the rear of the hospital. She
knows where to go and I can't wait to see her. She did
appear a bit fraught when I called her, maybe it's
because she, like me, has been on alert all day (it
wasn't and I will tell you about it later).

Freedom! The porter loads me, my drain, my
overnight bag and two large American style grocery
bags full of medicines and away we go. In no time at
all I am lost. We go through a maze of corridors and
across different concourses that join the various
buildings that have been added on over the years, it's

a very big hospital. I do my best to engage in conversation but it becomes apparent that the lady who is pushing me is limited in this field. She makes the effort to explain in bad English that she is Polish. We're there, the doors open and I get pushed out into the sunlight. Oh man, I can't tell you how good this feels, it's exhilarating to be outside, I can feel my mouth going dry and my eyes welling up. I call Michelle, she's hands free and says she is literally just turning into the entrance road for the collection area. We ring off. I look over to my right a little and I can see my car coming down the slope that leads from the rear of the BRI and where Oncology is based. It stops, why has it stopped? I can't see any other traffic. There's a guy in a hard hat and a high-vis jacket and he is talking to Michelle. What the bloody hell is going on? She calls and explains that the bottom of the slope has been dug up and she can't go any further. Give me bloody strength, I can see you for goodness sake. Ok I say, meet me around the front where we got dropped last Tuesday. I do my best to explain to my porter that the road is closed and no-one can get through. We need to go to the front of the building, the main reception. The words have not really hit home but with a series of hand gestures I think she has grasped what I am trying to explain. We are off again. I am furious, honestly, I was less than a 100 yards away, un-bloody-believable.

Back into the building, luckily we are not far from the front reception and in a couple of minutes we are there. I sit looking for the car, Michelle has had to navigate around a one-way system as there are roadworks everywhere, more bloody bicycle lanes I shouldn't wonder! She pulls up and both her and our youngest daughter get out. I can see by their faces they are both somewhat shocked to see the state I am in. They help me with all of my bags, get me out of the chair and on my feet. I wave goodbye to my porter and get helped into the front passenger seat of the car. Our chocolate brown Labrador has come along for the ride and she stands up on the back seat, wags her tail furiously and pops her head forward for a stroke and a peck. The girls come next and once we are all in, I say, "Let's go home."

They both agree on how done in I look, Michelle told me later she has never seen me look so small and helpless as I appeared sat in that wheelchair covered in bags. They are so happy to have me back and as we drive across the city centre to get to our side of town, they both recount the story of their day. It turns out Michelle decided have a major clean as I was coming home. Particularly the bathroom. She put some kind of solution into the sinks, its main purpose to break down hair as we have two daughters who both have long flowing locks and live in the bathroom! Anyway, to cut a long story short, this ended up having some sort of reaction with the bleach that had been poured previously. The youngest wandered in once it was empty to discover a similar scene to one of those 'baking soda volcano's' you come across at science fairs. It spilt out of the sink and was all over the floor with no sign of stopping. This was all happening between my sulky texts and phone calls and they were in panic mode as to how to stop it and clear it up before collecting me. Luckily one of our neighbours owns his own plumbing business and after Michelle called him, he got one of his boys to come around straight away and get it sorted. They literally had just finished clearing up before coming down for me now.

There was a lot of shouting going on so my daughter tells me, even the dog got some!

It's so nice to hear other voices and to have a chance to be part of a conversation, you can't believe how much I have missed this over the last 7 days. I ask my youngest what she has been up to and she happily fills me in. I can feel myself getting a bit choked and tears are starting to form. This has never happened to me before but out of nowhere I break down and start crying. I can see both of them are shocked, I utter almost comprehensibly, "I have had enough, I can't go through this again!" Michelle tries her best to comfort me and assures me it's all over. I feel awful, guilt is setting in, I should never have showed this weakness in front of my daughter. She sits quietly in the back of the car cuddling the dog and I apologise for being so silly, I don't know what came over me. We all have moist eyes now. The subject gets changed and I try to regroup as we complete the drive home.

Ironically, my statement of "I can't go through this again" actually turns out to be true and there will be more about that later.

Home, it's never looked so good. I get settled in and I am so happy it's untrue. My oldest daughter comes in from work and throws her arms around me to welcome me back. The girls are eager to know what the last 7 days have been like and I try my best to explain. They both express how awful it sounds and they all felt so guilty that they could not come in and see me and were here in the lovely sunshine getting on with their lives. I couldn't tell them about the lady in my ward and as I am recounting this now, I am not sure I have ever told anyone about my Saturday evening chat with the new doctor. Michelle is searching through all of my meds and is particularly concerned when she sees all of the hypodermic needles and a sharps box to put the empties in. I explain I will show her how to do it in the morning as I had to do my own today in order to get out and then she can do them every day until they run out. She seems quite pleased about this; I knew she would be. I lift my shirt so they can see where my drain is attached and also the new collection of scars I have across the left-hand side of my chest. I tell Michelle about the appointment on Thursday, hopefully they will take it out then. Excitement over, we phone for a celebration takeaway, it's Chinese again but what the hell. It's good to be back.

Michelle changes my dressing for the drain on the Wednesday, where the pipe joins my body really stings and looks red and angry. The pain is quite excruciating and I top up on some painkillers. It's difficult to find a comfy position either sitting or lying down so I don't get a great night's sleep. The letter is here for tomorrow's appointment and we have to be at the BRI clinic at ten-fifteen. Now, I thought I was going in to be checked by the consultant, have the drain removed and away we go. Got that wrong! Turns out his clinic is on a different floor in another building. He has been called away for an emergency so I am booked in for some tests that they can continue to do in his absence but I will not be able to leave until I have seen him. They explain that because of Covid, Michelle can't be here and so I tell her to go on home and I will call when I am done. The usual obs get done but on top of this I get weighed as well. I am taken to what looks like a six-bed ward with only a couple of beds in, luckily with an adjoining bathroom. I am placed in one of the tall visitor chairs and told hopefully it won't be too long. I explain that as I did not realise I was going to be here so long, I have not brought any of my extensive range of tablets with me. This concerns the nurse that is with me and she goes off to talk this through with one of the ward doctors. She returns with a wristband and explains that they have to admit me into the hospital again so that they can dispense drugs to me. They bring around some tea and biscuits and after a couple of hours, the man himself appears, all apologetic, arms splayed open and genuinely seems happy that I am still here. We exchange pleasantries and then get down to business. He pulls the curtain around us and asks me to lift my shirt. His examination is brief, he is happy with all of the results from earlier, he makes an adjustment on the drain after I complain about the discomfort and says that he is not ready to take it out. I am still leaking pancreatic juice and he wants us to record how much each day for another week. I am a little disappointed about this but let's just get it sorted. He makes an appointment on the spot for back at his consultancy room this time and I promise

153

to see him next week.

Boy was that a long week. The soreness from the pipe in my chest has now manifested itself as an infection which I just put up with as I am desperate to get this damn thing off. Michelle, bless her, empties the drain into a plastic measuring cup and records the volume as we were requested every day. Fair play to her, it isn't very pleasant. When I present myself back in front of the consultant a week later he is impressed enough to suggest it could now come off. I am smiling and nodding my approval as he gets up out of his seat and rummages around in one of his cabinets. Before I know it, he literally just rips it out and adds a small dressing to the wound. Job done! He is good enough to take a few questions as we discuss the possibility of the cancer returning. He says that I am in great shape considering what I have put my body through and hopefully will be strong enough for whatever manifests next. The reality is, due to the aggressive nature of my cancer, it is pretty much a certainty that it will be back, it's just a question of when. I know we are not supposed to but we shake hands and I thank him once more for everything he has done for me and my family. I walk out happy to be free of that damn drain, happy that I am free of this bloody disease again and looking forward to getting on with life, such as it is in these pandemic times. I am still here and whatever comes next, I will deal with.

It's halfway through June 2020 and this year's holiday plans are in ruins. We are supposed to be flying out to Singapore and then on to Bali in less than 6 weeks. There is a huge amount of confusion surrounding everyone's holiday plans and as much as I love travel, this time I feel I really need to get away, I have had enough. We end up having a couple of snatched days away in this country, just for a change of scene. It helps to clear my head a little as it is nice not to be in the same four walls but was not the same as going to a different country.

The end of August comes and goes and, frustratingly, I do not have a date for the 3 month scan I am due. I hit the phones and eventually I am assured a letter will be with me shortly. In just slightly less than a week, sure enough the appointment letter arrives. It's for the end of November! You have got to be kidding me? I am absolutely furious, I call the CT team in Southmead and somehow put my case across without having a fit. To placate me they offer an appointment at eight-thirty in the morning for the third Saturday in September and I readily accept. I am desperate to get the scan out of the way so I can get some normality and I can look at putting myself forward for a possible return to work in between the lockdowns that are being imposed on everyone. It feels like it's going to be a long three weeks waiting on the scan results.

October comes, with the CT scan done all we can do now is wait on the Consultant's call and hope that all is well.

JOURNEY FOUR – STAGE FOUR

It's 2 weeks away from Halloween and Covid-19 has come to town. For a few days, leading up to the October half term, Michelle has felt more than a little off colour. When her work ends on the Friday (she is in the education sector and works term-time only), the next nine days off, to re-charge her batteries, can't come fast enough. She continues to feel tired for the first couple of days but on the Tuesday gets a call from the NHS Track and Trace to say one of her colleagues had tested positive and for her to self-isolate for 7 days. She does as advised, returns to work on the day that she could, feeling fine and frustrated that her week off had been interrupted.

Two days later she has a terrible headache, her body aches all over, she's having hot flushes then is bitterly cold and a heavy fatigue sets in. She calls work and says she won't be in, feels a little stronger later in the day, calls 111 and they advise her to get a Covid test. She drives to our nearest drive-through test centre and Covid is confirmed 24 hours later. Bless her, it hits hard for the next couple of days (and we believe she still has some of the effects of this now) but we all muddle through to get her back on her feet as soon as we can. You can imagine how guilty she feels about not only bringing it into our household but possibly exposing me to it. To be fair, I have always said Covid is the least of my problems but we are sensible, keep our interaction to a minimum and I sleep on our sofa with the hound for the next 7 nights.

Now that this is over and she is all good we are sat in our living room staring at my phone waiting for the call. When it comes it's not good news. Introductions done, this time it is the Cancer Liaison Secretary who breaks the news to us. The cancer has reappeared and according to my latest scan, it has manifested itself in the bottom of my left lung and there is also an 'anomaly' in my lower chest wall on the same side. My case is now being passed on to the Oncology Department and they will be in touch with me shortly. She apologises once again for the bad news and we thank her for the call. I am really angry to think that if I had not chased up this latest scan, I would have been suffering this for at least another 2 months before being made aware of it and how much more damage could that have done? We both sit in shock and silence for a few moments, the tears well up and we really cannot believe it, I must have been a right horrible bastard in a previous life!

We share the news with the girls, they are stunned, "But Dad, it's been so quick this time." As per usual we 'circle the wagons' and just get on with it. I inform my boss who, again, is fantastic with his support and we spread the word amongst our family and friends. All we can do is wait. A letter arrives within a couple of days saying that I will have a telephone appointment with one of the consultants from Bristol Oncology, which is due at the end of the week, Friday at two p.m. Michelle and I are sat in my car waiting on the call which we will take hands free. The reason we have chosen to do this is because the youngest daughter is at home and we want to absorb the information we are about to receive first. The call comes and our latest consultant introduces herself. She is extremely sociable and we all participate in a thorough and lengthy discussion. She has studied my latest scan at length and informs us that the cancer that I now have is inoperable! This stops us both cold, "Does that mean I am terminal?" I blurt out. She gives a resounding, "No. You are not at that stage. It simply means that we are at the stage where chasing your cancer around with operations is no longer viable. As soon as one is removed another one appears. We will now tackle this from another angle. Right now, due to the advancement in medications over the last 5 years, we have a range of medicines that we can use to help contain the masses and, if we are lucky, even reverse them." She goes on to explain that having survived three stage three operations, two of those being within 9 months, that there is only so much trauma a body will put up with. As previously explained, neither chemotherapy nor radiotherapy will be an option, so the plan is to start with a relatively new treatment called Targeted Therapy. This will be a course of medicine to be taken daily until directed otherwise. We talk about the other daily tablets that I'm on for my pancreas and are assured that they will not conflict with one another. Once all of our questions are answered she informs us that she will contact the pharmacy and organise the tablets and include some other items that I may need to offset possible side effects that I may experience from these really strong medicines that she is dispensing. Before she rings off, she gives us a 24 hour emergency phone number to use if needed and asks us to arrange for a set of blood samples from our local doctors surgery. She will want bloods taken every 2 weeks for the next 2 months and will book my next CT scan for January 2021 and a consultant call 2 weeks after. My CT scans will now be moved up to every 3 months. She gives us another phone number which is for two members of her team who share their role. They will liaise with me and inform me if there are any immediate issues with the blood samples or whether they are all ok. She wishes us well and rings off. Luckily Michelle has been scribbling everything down, it's a lot to take in.

So, now I am having to live with stage four cancer. It's frustrating but hey, I am still here. My prophecy, of I can't do any more operations, has come true. The pharmacy calls and informs me of the delivery, it will come directly to our home and they are checking that I or somebody responsible will be there to take it in. When it arrives, it has several contents. Apart from several boxes of the drug that I am to take daily, there is a moisturiser cream and a mouthwash in there. How bizarre. We look at the tablets and pull the information sheet from within the box. It's all in very small writing and we scan it, looking for any other information that we think we should be aware of. In the bottom of the bag is a folded sheet of typed A4. This is what we were after, the known side effects. The sheet is quite extensive. I will just give you the highlights: mouth ulcers (hence the mouthwash), nausea, fatigue, high blood pressure, skin irritation - targeting the palms of the hands and souls of the feet, kidney damage, liver damage, diarrhoea, sepsis, thyroid issues and skin and hair pigmentation changes. Lucky me!

I start the treatment the very next day. Once I have taken the two tablets, I am not allowed to eat anything for at least 2 hours. I have a routine in place now and I generally take them between 5.30 and 6 a.m. Luckily, I am not much of a breakfast person so it does not really affect me. Right now, as I write this I have been on this therapy regime for around 6 months. Of all of the horrible side effects that were listed I have suffered from high blood pressure, that's finished with though now, I occasionally suffer from diarrhoea, I had an occasion over the Christmas period where my bloods showed my liver was being damaged and my white cells were off the chart. I still get quite a bit of fatigue which is totally debilitating, let me tell you, and the strangest side effect that has happened was my lovely rich dark brown (only slightly speckled with grey!) hair complete with my more salt than pepper beard and moustache went white literally overnight! I joke that I now look like a cross between Father Christmas and Captain Birdseye. When I first started doing the bloods at my doctors surgery I asked about whether I should be having the Covid jab instead of waiting for the vaccination rollout. After the screen notes were checked and I responded in the negative to any breathing issues I was told if I hadn't been issued a letter by the government then no. I was ok with this but both Michelle and the girls were incensed by it.

We get to 2021 (the present year), the two contacts from Oncology have been keeping in touch with me, advising on how my blood levels are looking and warning me when the liver issue was identified. As promised, I get an appointment sent through for my next CT scan, it's for a couple of weeks' time, around the end of January and it's to be done at the BRI. I have to look twice as I have only ever had scans at Southmead. No, I read it right, it is indeed at the BRI. The day of the scan comes, the building that it is in is quite old, it's a real fifties-sixties style office building, retro décor and really old furniture. Despite the ongoing Covid restrictions I am surprised at just how many people are milling about waiting for scans and x-rays, all trying to keep 2 metres apart as per the posters and floor stickers placed all over. I manage to find a seat and wait for my turn. My name is called and off we go again. I follow the nurse directly into the scanner room. Introductions are made and the radiologist asks me if I have had one before, I nod and explain this is number eleven! She asks me to remove my coat, belt and shoes and hop onto the bed. I challenge this and ask, "Do you not want me to change?" Apparently, there is no need to worry about that. A cannula gets put into my left arm for the 'with contrast' and scan number eleven gets under way. Back at home Michelle is intrigued by how different an experience that was compared to all of my previous scans.

The next couple of weeks whilst waiting on the consultant pass pretty slowly as they always do. The call comes, we are sat in our lounge staring at my phone and she tells us the latest results. The tumour in my lung has shrunk by almost 30 percent, great news and proof that the pills are doing what they are designed to do. We sit looking at each other in utter relief, this makes a nice change, perhaps at last we have turned a corner. We discuss how the pills are affecting me and it is mutually agreed that while I am still off work I should continue to take the maximum dose in order to continue the good that has been achieved so far. So, it continues. As she is about to ring off Michelle mentions my waiting for my Covid jab. "What do you mean you haven't had your jab? You should have had it back in November as you're in the Critical Illness Category." More screen checking on her end, turns out I was missed off the list. The government letter arrives 2 days later and I get my first jab at the end of that week!

My routine is wake early, take my 'anti-cancer' pills as I call them and then, depending on how I feel a little later, I am either up and about around 8/8.30 a.m. or it can be more like 11. There are still days, unfortunately, when I don't get up at all. Once up, I have a cup of tea, dunk a couple of biscuits (my normal breakfast fare) and, of course, share with the hound who is always on my bed in the mornings, it is literally Michelle out and the dog in. Where I can, I help out with my youngest, giving her lifts as she is at college and her timetable looks like a bingo card! I walk the dog, not too far as she is knocking on a bit, almost twelve which is a decent age for a chunky chocolate Labrador. I put out the washing, I iron if there is anything that needs doing, I go food shopping when needed, I do my best to keep the house clean and up together and I cook. Luckily, I can do all of these things and I try to fill my days so that I am not bored out of my head. Michelle is at work all week, it's not fair for her to have to wade through all of this especially when I am home all of the time. To be fair she does her bit, always finds little things that I have missed (hey, I am a bloke, sue me!) and when I am bedridden and feeling grotty, she swings into action. We have a lot of fresh food, all cooked by my fair hands daily. The girls agree that our diet has never been so good but as I explain to them, it's because I have the time to prepare all of these fresh ingredients. Normally, Michelle would be walking through the door around five and with me supposed to be working at our branch in Weston-Super-Mare (my choice) I probably won't be home until around seven. Nobody wants to spend an hour and a half plus prepping and cooking, it will be so late by the time you actually get around to eat. On top of this I call my doctors once a month for an update to

my 'doctor's note', book the odd blood test when I
am asked to and wait on my next 3 month scan.

We get past Easter, which is early this year, and I
get a phone appointment with the Chief Pharmacist at
the BRI. I am taken by surprise by this but I make the
appointment as planned. She comes across as very
friendly and we easily slip into a good chat about how
I am getting on with the meds and coping with the
dosage. I am told that it is rare for somebody to be on
the highest dose for more than a couple of months
but the longer I can cope with it the better chance of
it succeeding, at least in the first instance. She is
happy with what we have discussed and promises to
add to the notes for my consultant. I tell her that I am
expecting the appointment for my next CT scan and
she says she will mention it to the Oncology
department. I wait every day for the letter to arrive
and as we get towards the end of the month it still
isn't here. I call the number that I have for the nurses
that deal with my bloods and things, and manage to
get a hold of one of them. She promises that she will
look into it and comes back to me the next day. It's in

the post, be with me in a day or two. I thank her for this although in reality I am a bit miffed that I have had to chase this up yet again. The appointment arrives, it's for the following week at the Spire Private Hospital. Wow, I haven't been here since I waved my right kidney goodbye. To my mind I have been clearly missed again, as I was expecting to return to the BRI for a scan like the last time but it appears to me I have been panic booked into a private hospital after bringing it to their attention yet again, where they obviously have a space at a premium, no doubt at the cost of the NHS.

THE NEXT JOURNEY – FIVE ALIVE (FOR NOW!)

It's a week exactly since the CT scan. I have had no letter from Oncology stating when I will talk to the consultant. I pick up the phone and make the call, again! I leave a message on the contact phone number I have. As per the message, I get a call back within the hour. I explain that as I have no letter, I do not know when to arrange the next set of bloods that they always insist on. A promise is made to get back to me as quickly as possible, she needs to speak to my consultant. The following day I get a call, whilst sitting in my car waiting on my youngest to come out of college, from a chap whose name I instantly forget saying that my consultant appointment will be tomorrow (Friday) at 2.30 p.m.

I immediately think to myself, shit; I am in trouble. The fact that it's the next day and there was no mention of me arranging bloods, I know there is something up. I text Michelle at work so she can arrange an hour out the next day because I know she will want to be there, no matter what. When she gets home later, we discuss it and as much as she wants to argue with my theory, she knows deep down I am probably right.

Not very often will you hear me say this but I hate being right! The consultant starts with an apology, someone has left her department and they are a little behind. Here comes the 'sandwich' effect. "So, great news, the cancer in your chest wall has gone." Michelle and I both look at one another in total shock. "That's brilliant," we both say at pretty much the same time. She confirms that the one in my lung has not grown any more since it shrank by 30 percent on my last scan. "Wow, thank you so much," we both chime in. Then, "The latest scan shows (here we go!) a 2.6 centimetre lesion of some sort on your upper abdomen, we are not sure at this stage exactly what it is but our first thoughts are that it is connected to your earlier kidney cancer." We exchange glances again – really, bloody hell! She goes on to explain they want me in again for another scan, she is arranging one for me in about a month's time as I have only just had one. She wants me to arrange for some bloods as soon as I can and I tell her that I will organise it as asked. My case will be discussed next Friday with the entire team as to the best way to proceed. Michelle hits her with the all important question, in reality what next? If it is another cancer, technically number six in just over 6 years, there are other drugs that I can switch to on the Targeted Therapy and there is also something called Immunisation Therapy that I could cross over to and that could manifest itself as a daily mixture of tablets and a monthly visit to Oncology for an hour's worth of an intravenous drip full of goodies!

And that's where I am now. Waiting for the next journey to begin.

EPILOGUE(ISH)

Quite fitting really, the word epilogue is Greek for conclusion. So much of what you get told when you are facing cancer is, to coin a phrase, "all Greek to me". It's a great saying, not really fitting as an end here though because I am still not near a conclusion, which I suppose in reality will eventually come in the form of a terminal diagnosis, something I have accepted but that is a way down the line, I hope.

When I decided to eventually write this book (I had been thinking about doing something for some time), it was in my head to write a short piece to give an insight as to what you might expect to experience so that you would feel a little less overwhelmed and a bit more in control if you had recently been diagnosed with cancer. I wanted to try and break it down a bit and for it not to be so scary, that was my initial aim. I also wanted to leave some form of legacy not only for my two beautiful daughters to hopefully one day pass on to their children so that they might have an idea of what their grandfather was like. Also, by having some of any profit generated from these recollections to go to the Cancer Research UK charity to help them so that one day they will be able to beat this and other families won't have to suffer through this horrible disease.

Once I started writing I just remembered more and more, and it opened the floodgates to something much bigger than I realised and took off in a totally different direction. It became very therapeutic to be able to put it all down in print and it was only once I started to proofread it that I realised what a journey my family and I have been on over the last 6 years. I would like to stress that every word I have written is true. I have not embellished it in any way and I have made no effort to make any part of it comical although some of it clearly is. It all happened exactly as described, exactly.

There have been times writing this when I have been completely overcome with emotion. I have read snippets out to Michelle for her opinion and had her in tears and now I have decided to bring it to a conclusion here, I am actually a little sad. In a strange way it feels almost like the end. I now know I have another journey in front of me but I want to tell the tale in reality while I still can. It is important that it is in my words. I have been home since the twenty-fourth of March 2020, that's a year and 3 months at the time of finishing this project. I have been writing almost daily for over 8 weeks and once I started it became almost compulsive and I wrote virtually every day apart from those that I was bed-ridden.

Remember me describing how my dad was a 'man's man'? Well I have always strived to be like him, it's how my brother and I were brought up, to know the difference between right and wrong, to be strong, to not show weakness, not to suffer fools gladly and to help those who could not help themselves. With him in mind and the terrible mistake he made of not recognising his cancer earlier, it turned out to be the last lesson he taught the both of us and hence the title of this book was born. I never thought I would ever bear my soul like I have in this book. It wouldn't have entered my head that I could feel so low and lonely as I did when I was in ITU, that's just not me. I would never have cried in front of Michelle and our daughters, that's weak and not in the handbook. As far as I can remember I have only ever cried a couple of times in my life and that's when my dad died and when one of my best friends told me about his prostate cancer, both of these cut through me like a knife. This disease has changed me so very much as a person. I used to sweat the small things and take stuff for granted, now I am much more tolerant, not just of myself but also of others. The small things don't worry me at all anymore and I look at all the good things that were right in front me and embrace them because despite all of the odds I am still here to do so.

I have been massively lucky to have the unending support of my beautiful wife and two fabulous daughters and I want apologise to them for all of the heartbreak that I have unwittingly caused. To thank them for their never waning support and their love for me. My medical team from all of the departments (I am working my way through the majority of them!) have been fantastic, including my own GP surgery who initially recognised that there was a potentially a problem, and to my GP in particular, who has been massively supportive to me and my family and continues to be so. To think that these people have been on the front line and under a huge amount of stress with an unthinkable pandemic and still managed to make time for me from a blood test to an operation and the continuation of aftercare is humbling. But all of these wonderful people are only human, they have a hundred and one things to do and their systems are often at full stretch and overwhelmed. I have shown on several occasions that you too have to play your part. I have had scans not booked when they should have been, consultant appointments not scheduled, my first pre-op missed which could have been fatal, and then completely missed off of the critically vulnerable list in regard to the Covid-19 jab, again this could have been a complete disaster from a health point of view for my family and me. Can you imagine if Michelle or the girls had passed this on to me and I had died from it? I know that this horrible scenario has happened for families around the whole world, you can't begin to imagine what that kind of guilt must feel like. That could have been my family!

If you are reading this and you recently have been diagnosed with cancer, you have my utter sympathy. I want you to bear in mind that not everyone is unlucky enough to go on an extended journey like I have. I was only reading last week the advances in medicine that have been made for renal cell carcinoma and how these are now dispensed immediately after the operation itself which greatly reduces the chance of the cancer ever returning. Not available 5 years ago sadly, but a great advancement for people now.

My advice, for what it is worth, is to keep your chin up, there is no point in burying your head in the sand or being miserable about it and feeling sorry for yourself. You can't worry about something until it happens. I genuinely believe the more positive you remain, the better your chances. Tomorrow comes just the same. The other thing relates to one of the paragraphs above. If you have been given a date of when something should happen or you should have had a letter or a call and you have not received it, phone them. Chase them. Don't feel bad about it, these wonderful people are dealing with hundreds if not thousands of patients and while I don't think I am any more important than anyone else, I think I have managed to highlight that the system can miss you out and that in reality it could cost you your life.

As I wind this up I want to draw your attention to the Cancer Research adverts that you see on TV. I still remember the advert on ITV when I was a little child growing up in the early seventies, as there were only three TV channels then, with four children running and playing in a forest with the sunlight bursting through. They all sit on a fallen tree and a voice over announces that one in four of these children will see cancer in their lifetime. In the nineties it was a similar advert now stating one in three. Now it's one in two, which realistically means everyone. It makes sense that in reality every other person on the planet is going to get some form of cancer in their lifetime. If you're the unlucky one that has the cancer then surely the other one is a loved one and, believe you me, it can be just as devastating for them as it can be for you, sometimes more so. Just remember it's your life, you only get one go at it. For your sake and the sake of your family and your loved ones, take it by the horns, smile, don't take it personally or make those around you miserable, make the most of your time because I can honestly tell you I have made the most of mine.

Good luck to you all.

ANY LAST WORDS?
(AN ADDED FOOTNOTE)

Since finishing my story I have been trudging through the minefield of trying to find the correct publishing house (done, hopefully!). I have had a couple more things happen that are relative to my story and I thought I should share.

I found out on the actual payday in July 2021 that my employer has decided to abandon me. I received a phone call literally 2 hours before my monthly pay was about to land in my bank account to say that the company had made the decision to no longer support me financially, the payment I was about to receive would be substantially less than I had previously been paid. As from August 2021 I will be on SSP only, which I believe is £96.35 a week, which they legally have to pay me for a maximum of 28 weeks then nothing further after that!

To say I was shocked was an understatement. The support that has been shown to me by the company over the incredibly difficult times for my family and myself has been incredible and I have been hugely grateful to them for it. I understand that while I have been away some changes at the top in head office have occurred and I am now being cast aside.

After 9 years of professionally representing the company, putting the brand and its business needs as a priority, being recognised as an employee who gave great service and had a high retention of customers, this is a real smack in the face to me personally. When I think of all of the hours, late evenings, weekends and bank holidays I have put in, to be cast to one side like this has made me feel unimportant, unwanted and more than a little foolish. Going back to work and having some normality in my life was one of the goals I had set and this now feels like it has been taken away from me. I have no desire at all to work for a company that has no value in their staff, it sets a tone with me that I think is disgusting and I certainly don't relish the thought of working under these clinical, uncaring, all about the top line and profit egomaniacs. As angry as this made me and as frustrating as this is I will continue to act in a professional capacity and look to support my family.

Oh well, just another thing for me to deal with – don't worry, I will!

On another note, I have recently spoken to the consultant. Although there is an addition in my abdomen it appears my Targeted Therapy is working well and currently keeping all three tumours at bay. Although, just to add to the consistency, the consultant assured me that the BRI Pharmacy would be sending me my next 3 month batch of what I call my 'anti-cancer' tablets and after a week of no delivery, I decided to call the pharmacy to see where they were. It turns out that no prescription had been passed to them from Oncology, hence no delivery and so once again I have had to chase it all up. Just goes to prove what I said earlier! Keep chasing!

After all of this I have one last piece of advice for you all and it's this:

If you recognise me and I am standing in a queue for the Lottery, stand directly behind me!

ACKNOWLEDGMENTS

Professional Acknowledgements:

Dr Mark Wright MD FRCS (1965 – 2017) – Consultant/Urological Surgeon

Urology Department, Southmead Hospital – North Bristol NHS Trust

Dr Huw Taylor MBChB BSc Hons MRCGP

All Staff at Cadbury Heath Health Centre that have continued with my after care

Bristol Royal Infirmary Cardiothoracic Team

Mr Stijn Van Laarhoven – Locum Consultant Hepatopancreatobiliary Surgeon

Bristol Royal Infirmary ITU Department

Dr Susan Masson – Bristol Haematology & Oncology Centre & her team

Macmillan Cancer Support – www.macmillan.org.uk

Cancer Research UK – www.cancerresearchuk.org

Matthew Worsley, Stuart Payne & Richard Broady – past and present management team Drive Motor Retail

George Wolfe – Independent Financial Advisor – The Medical Partnership

Nicky Marshall and Sharon Critchlow – Directors & Publishers – www.discoveryourbounce.com

Mark Guatieri – Cover Artist – www.brand51.co.uk

Personal Acknowledgements:

Heartfelt thanks to all of our close friends and family members that have continued to show their support not only to me, but in my mind and much more importantly, to Michelle and the girls over what has been a difficult period for us all. Luckily for us there are too many of you to mention here! Thanks again.

My wonderful, caring, long suffering wife Michelle and our two beautiful daughters India and Erin (see, you both got a mention at last!). Without all of your unending support and love I would not have found the strength to get my ass out of bed and fight this thing. Because of you all, I make the most of every day and promise to continue to do so. Love you.

Last, but in no means least, my ever present, ever faithful chocolate brown Labrador 'Buttons', always there for us all (especially if you have food!).
If I have missed anyone please don't take it personally, I don't!

"Tomorrow comes, just the same"

Nicholas Collins - 2021